S0-EIC-800

DOCTOR JESUS
Still Performs
MIRACLES

Warren Sears

DOCTOR JESUS

Still Performs
MIRACLES

G. WARREN SEARS

YAV PUBLICATIONS
ASHEVILLE, NORTH CAROLINA

Copyright © 2013 by G. Warren Sears

All rights reserved. No part of this book shall be reproduced or transmitted
in any form or by any means, electronic, mechanical, magnetic, photographic
including photo-copying, recording, or by any information storage and retrieval
system, without prior written permission of the publisher. No patent liability is
assumed with respect to the use of the information contained herein. Although
every precaution has been taken in the preparation of this book, the publisher and
author assume no responsibility for errors or omissions. Neither is any liability
assumed for damages resulting from the use of the information contained herein.

First Edition

ISBN: 978-1-937449-26-1

Published by:

YAV PUBLICATIONS
ASHEVILLE, NORTH CAROLINA

YAV books may be purchased in bulk for educational, business,
fund-raising, or sales promotional use. For information, contact
Books@yav.com or phone toll-free 888-693-9365.

Visit our website: www.InterestingWriting.com

3 5 7 9 10 8 6 4 2
Assembled in the United States of America
Published November 2013

Contents

Acknowledgments

During the process of writing this book, I have realized — more than ever — how blessed I am to be a member of the family of God. At every step of the way, I have so much enjoyed the help, encouragement, and prayers of Christian friends — too numerous to name them all! But allow me to express my profound thanks to the following for their generous help with this book:

George Cupp. The idea for this book was born when he told me the amazing story of his son's miraculous recovery from a motorcycle accident. Wendy Agard, for her enthusiastic support and outstanding proofreading. To the experts at the Apple Store in Annapolis, and Wendy's friend, Margaret Whitlock — for their assistance with technical challenges. To Brenda Sears, my daughter-in-law, for her uncanny ability to fix my computer when it does something weird, thus saving me trips to Annapolis. To my son, Steve Sears, for helping me equip my in-house studio. To Lois Fitzpatrick for telling me about the Cardens' miracle baby. To Don Richardson, George Rossier, and Carl Jorgensen — beloved prayer partners. To Marlene Cleveland for introducing me to other prospects for stories. To Jim and Betty Priddy, for telling me about Ron Baule's unbelievable experience. To Amy Deardon, an enormous encourager and advisor who is the fearless leader of the Third-Saturday-of-the-Month Christian Writers Group, where I met Chris — Chris Yavelow, a dear friend, advisor, and the publisher of this book. Most of all, my special thanks to the sixteen trusting souls who graciously gave me permission to share their testimonies.

If there be any glory, may it all go to our Lord and Savior, Jesus Christ.

Foreword

If you like inspiring, life-changing stories, then you have just picked up the right book. It's no coincidence that this riveting compilation of testimonies can be credited to one whose life story is full of inspiration and encouragement. Warren Sears, aided by God's amazing grace, has put together a fascinating book of modern-day miracles.

As you open this book, consider yourself indeed fortunate to be privy to situations and circumstances that have changed the course of these people's lives, forever. These accounts remind us that God has pulled out all the stops to capture our attention. You may have had miracles in your life as amazing as these, or even more so, but you never saw them as wake-up calls. This book is a sobering reminder that nothing in life happens without a reason, but all things have eternal consequences.

You will be especially intrigued by the stories of people snatched from the clutches of certain death and given a new perspective on life. These heart-warming true stories will make you sit up and pay attention. No longer will you take today or tomorrow for granted, but will enter each day looking for and recognizing the miracles in life.

I'm thankful to Warren for taking time to listen to and record these narratives so that others, like me, are able to share in the triumph of these special men and women.

—Pastor Tyrone King

Introduction

People. Jesus loves people—all people! He is just as willing to heal us today as He was when He personally walked by the Sea of Galilee. Why should that surprise us? After all, the Bible tells us, "God is love," and "Jesus is the same, yesterday, today and tomorrow." So, get ready for a powerful boost of faith.

The people you'll meet in these pages have high hopes that their stories will give readers a faith-lift. They want you to receive the kind of faith (peaceful trust) that will not only heal your body and soul, but will place you safely in that convoy to heaven when the Lord Jesus Christ comes again.

These stories demonstrate the awesome power of prayer. Many readers will identify with someone in these stories. For example, anyone who reads the story of George Cupp, Jr. will be inspired to read scripture aloud to a loved one even while he is in a coma. A pregnant woman will be greatly encouraged by the story of Tiny Tim who was born premature, weighing less than two pounds at birth! The story of Damon Journee will encourage mothers to pray for their children, even the ones who *seem* hopeless. That child—under satanic influence, with a body ripped-through by seventeen bullets—is not beyond God's reach. Someone with multiple sclerosis will be encouraged by Dave Harman's miracle! A woman with chronic pain will take heart when she reads the miraculous story of Bobby Mammen.

These stories include a variety of miracles. In a few cases, it was the Lord, "Doctor Jesus," working alone, who pushed aside the enemy. In other cases, it was the teamwork of down-to-earth doctors and nurses used by Jesus to facilitate healing. Medical professionals did not always offer hope. In these real stories, some actually pronounced patients dead. However, the miracles had one thing in common: Someone was calling on Doctor Jesus.

Countless mysteries are associated with the subject of divine healing. No one understands why God heals some people, but not others; or why God allows some faithful Christians to suffer, yet He often seems to bless the lives of unbelievers. We just need to acknowledge that God's ways are higher than ours, and these mysteries are simply beyond our understanding. How can we possibly understand the One who created the whole universe; everything that lives; everything that breathes? One thing we know for sure: God loves us more than we can imagine, and He has a wonderful purpose for our lives when we put our lives in His hands.

As we study the examples of Jesus healing various people in the Bible, we learn that the key is *faith*. Some were healed because of their personal faith; some were healed by the faith of Jesus or His disciples; and some were healed by the faith of a loved one. These same principles hold true today.

A wonderful thing is, faith itself is a *spiritual gift* from God. So if we are weak in faith, we can ask God to increase our faith...and He will. For example: Consider the biblical story of Doubting Thomas, who was not with the other disciples when Jesus appeared to them (the first time) after His resurrection. Thomas said, "Unless I see in His hands, the print of the nails, I will not believe." When He appeared again to them in the upper room, the first one Jesus approached was Thomas. "Reach here with your finger," said the Lord, "and see My hands; and reach here your hand and put it into My side; and do not be unbelieving, but believing." (John 20:27)

I'm also thankful for the example of the Apostle Paul's "thorn in the flesh." By this we know that God may choose not to heal everyone in this life.

(II Corinthians 12:7-9). God's words to Paul were, "My grace is sufficient for thee: for My strength is made perfect in weakness." The ultimate healing will come when believers are given a new body in heaven.

A personal note

I had given up the idea of ever writing another book. But when George Cupp, Sr. (a dear friend for some forty years) told me the details of his son's experience—WOW! It was so incredible. I said to myself, "This story needs to be told to everyone!" It had been reported originally in a small country newspaper in Brandywine, Maryland, but that didn't reach enough people. The world needs to hear that Jesus Christ still performs miracles!

Shortly after that, God arranged for me to meet Wendy Agard. She was visiting my church one day. I told her George's story, and she agreed that it needed to be published. Not only that, Wendy wonderfully agreed to work with me as an assistant and proofreader. The amazing thing (I discovered later) is that Wendy is a trained nurse. So she was well qualified to advise on medical terminology. Only God could have arranged our meeting.

Naturally, when we began telling others about the book, more stories of miracles soon came our way. Most came from Christians; some from our church, and some from Christian friends from different denominations.

Although some expressions of the Holy Spirit in these stories may seem strange to some readers, I know that God can do anything He wants to. Therefore, I've simply told the stories just as they were told to us, with little attempt to analyze or explain. Nevertheless, in some cases (in order to achieve clarity) I obtained permission to make a few minor changes in grammar and sentence structure.

The stories are true, in so far as memories and medical records are reliable. They are all so unbelievable that I was careful to include documented, verifiable information—such as names of hospitals, places, dates, and other important details.

I had the pleasure of becoming acquainted with everyone, either in person or through cyber-space. They are all happy to know that their stories may help others to receive more faith in God, and to show you that our wonderful Lord Jesus is alive and active in the world today! And always, only a prayer away.

My prayer for you

I earnestly pray that every reader will fall in love with Jesus and, if they have never done so, will receive the greatest miracle of all—as Jesus said, "You must be born again." (ST. JOHN 3:3-8) How? Simply confess your sins to God, and ask Him to forgive you and fill you with the Holy Spirit, so that you may live a life that is pleasing to Him. You can talk to Him anytime, any place. He's on duty 24/7, and He is a good Listener.

Now, we have God's promise that whatever happens to His children in this world, the Lord will give us His peace that passes understanding, and we shall dwell in the house of the Lord, forever.

—*G. Warren Sears*

The Story of
George Cupp, Jr.

As told by George Cupp, Sr.

Dr. Patel cried. He cried the day we left.

It was a Friday afternoon. George, Jr. had bought a motorcycle some months before. I wasn't happy about it. I never did like motorcycles. Thankfully, he had met a man who was willing to trade his car for the bike, and they had made a 4 o'clock appointment to make the swap that very day. Shortly before 4 p.m., Danny Bottler, our neighbors' 20 year-old son, asked George to take him for one last ride.

We didn't have cell phones in those days. My boss was the one who answered the phone, and he called me to his desk. It was my oldest son, Wayne, on the line. "Dad!" he blurted out. "George and Danny have been in a very bad accident. YOU'D BETTER COME RIGHT AWAY. Dad, one of them is dead; cut in half! I think it's Danny."

As I headed home, my heart pounded with dread and fear. I fought that all-too-familiar feeling in the pit of my stomach. My gut was telling me that 21 year-old George, Jr., was either dead or dying.

Pulling up at the scene, I barely stepped out of the car before the facts starting flying at me in a whirlwind; bits and pieces of horrific information. Because of the nature of the accident, Danny had died instantly. His youthful body — catapulted through the air — had hit a taut, transverse wire (extending from a telephone pole). Paramedics said that George wasn't going to live, either.

I couldn't process this — the impending doom of losing another child. My knees felt like jelly. My mind, though numb, was processing data at record speed. I remember falling to my knees and crying out to God. I pled with Him; begged Him, "God, don't let my son die! Please don't let my son die! God, do you see my son?"

And then something amazing happened. This was one of the few times that I literally heard God speak to me. I heard His voice, distinctly. He said, "Yes. Do you see My Son?"

Immediately, in my mind's eye, I saw Jesus — beaten beyond recognition; nailed to the cross; taking the punishment for our sins. At that moment, a strange peace came over me. Knowing that Jesus has the power over life and death, the calm I experienced was the peace of God that is beyond my understanding. I knew God was with me.

George had been airlifted to the Prince George's General Hospital, Shock Trauma in Cheverly, Maryland. I asked one of the nurses in the Emergency Department (ED) if she was a Christian. Indeed, she was. This was comforting, but I couldn't understand why all these nurses wouldn't look at me. Whenever their gaze bumped into mine, they would quickly look away. Finally, I approached this Christian nurse and asked her, "How is he, nurse? How's my son?" She looked at me with a professional blend of love, sympathy, and reservation. "It's all up to God," she said. That's all she was willing and able to say. Days later, some of the nurses explained to me that they couldn't bring themselves to look at me, that dreadful evening, because they were certain my son was not going to live.

Another Christian nurse described the experience of removing George's MAST trousers in the ED. The only way she could keep the doctors and nurses from slipping and sliding in all that blood was to spread blankets on the floor. Working on him relentlessly, they transfused him with nine pints of blood. Initially, he had no blood pressure, no pulse, and his pupils were dilated and non-reactive. My son had been clinically dead.

When the police asked one of the doctors about the status of the driver, the doctor, convinced that it was impossible for this patient to survive, reported that George Cupp, Jr. was dead. Consequently, the local newspaper printed that both boys had died in that fatal motorcycle accident, September 7, 1984.

My wife, Wayne, and I had been in the waiting room for about two hours — praying over and over again — when we saw them wheel him by (about 30 feet away). But I didn't recognize him. The son I knew had been an amateur boxer, 6' 2"and 195 pounds. All three of us — Wayne, George,Jr. and I, have been inducted into the Washington, D.C. Boxing Hall of Fame. People were always predicting that George was going to be the heavyweight champion of the world. This young man appeared to weigh close to 300 pounds. They had shaved off his hair, and his head was all bloated up. He had sustained seventy-two bone fractures. He had broken both hips; both of his shoulders; his clavicle (collar bone); all of the ribs on his left side; at least a dozen bones in his back; his sternum (breast bone); and his pelvis. His thigh bones had been snapped in half. Reportedly, bits of grass from somebody's mangled lawn were clinging to the jagged stubs of his fractured femurs. There'd also been a compound fracture of his tibia; the bone jutting through his skin. His spleen was ruptured; one lung had collapsed at the scene (the other, later, in the hospital) his liver was lacerated; his pancreas was smashed; and there were four intracranial hemorrhages. Both his esophagus and bronchi were lacerated.

There were three shock trauma surgeons assigned to his case. Their immediate assessment had been, "No hope." But they operated, anyway. Another ten hours passed before they allowed me to visit him. This stranger, my son, was comatose with tubes in his mouth and nose, and rubber tubing exiting from between his ribs. Though on life support, he was "Stable at this moment," the doctor explained. That was all he could say.

He gave me the grave prognosis a little later: "George will die tonight. He cannot possibly live."

The next morning, September 8, 1984, down here in Brandywine, neighbors read the morning paper and came over to express their condolences. Though grateful for these expressions of love and concern, I clung to the Lord to sustain my faith and sanity, and quickly learned to reply, "If my son is dead, this is news to me."

The police came out and took measurements. They weighed everything, and calculated that George had been going about fifty-five miles per hour when the accident occurred. Danny had to have launched out of his seat by about eighteen inches, or so, in order to be severed the way he was. The officers were puzzled. "We don't know why or how that same cable didn't hit your son," they said. I just listened. I listened and marveled. I don't understand, but I know some day I will. The main thing, in all of this, is to give God glory.

George hung on for hours. Hours grew into days. Then days became weeks. During week two, I was approached by a liaison nurse. "I've noticed, Mr. Cupp, that you've been kind of living at the hospital. You don't leave here till 2:00 or 3:00 in the morning. That's too long for you to be here."

"My boss is very gracious," I said. "He lets me off every day about 2 o'clock. Remember when I first came here?" I continued. "I said to you, 'With all due respect, do you have any children?' You said, 'No.' So I said, 'I don't expect you to comprehend this, but that's my son in there. The doctors said they have done all they can do...and they said the rest is up to God. That's what the nurses told me.' So I've said, 'I'm not leaving this hospital. I want to read God's word to him. In Psalm 107, verse 20, the Word says, 'He sent His Word and healed them and saved them from their destructions.' So every night the nurses have let me come in here and read the Bible to George, and talk to him; pat him; touch him." I appreciated the lady's concern, but she had to know that I was firmly resolved to stay the course.

I kept my Bible with me at all times. Over and over again, I just kept reading scripture to George; like Isaiah 41:10: "Fear thou not; for I am with thee: be not dismayed; for I am thy God: I will strengthen thee; yea, I will help thee; yea, I will uphold thee with the right hand of my righteousness." Fear not! And another favorite starts in Isaiah 40:28: "Hast thou not known? hast thou not heard, that the everlasting God, the LORD, the Creator of the ends of the earth, fainteth not, neither is weary? there is no searching of his understanding. He giveth power to the faint; and to them that have no might he increaseth strength. Even the youths shall faint and be weary, and the young men shall utterly fall: But they that wait upon the LORD shall renew their strength; they shall mount up with wings as eagles; they shall run, and not be weary; and they shall walk, and not faint."

I knew the doctors had done all they could do. I knew that it was up to God. God says His Word heals! So I kept reading portions of God's Word to my son every night.

Amazed that he continued to live, the critical care team expertly cared for George, faithfully tending to my precious son's limp and shattered body. A high-tech rotating bed ensured that George was turned regularly. Every night, the staff allowed me to visit him. He was in a coma for about 30 days. On approximately day 29, his mother and I walked in, and the whole thing hit her like a ton of bricks. "He might as well be dead." Gathering the remaining fragile strings of her bleeding, broken heart, she turned on her heel and walked out.

George was septic; had developed an infection on his brain; had contracted pneumonia; and was lying on ice blankets to reduce a fever that wouldn't break. His temperature was 106 degrees, at times, but they couldn't find the source of the infection.

I saw George's doctor frequently. He gave me his honest assessment. "If your son lives," he said, "he will be vegetative." He took me to a ward in the hospital where there were about a dozen patients just lying there with their mouths hanging open. He was preparing me, I suppose, for a future with a loved one who would never wake up.

George's legs were huge and they kept bleeding through the bandages, so they changed the dressings repeatedly. But they didn't set the bones in his legs until the sixth week. The doctors explained to me about inflammation of the brain, and the hemorrhages. They didn't set his legs because the legs were low priority. "The brain injuries can kill him," they had said. "We can fix the legs later."

During our first two weeks, there was an Indian doctor on George's team. He wore a turban; he was Sikh. Two months later, I was in the lunchroom (with my Bible by my side) and the same Sikh doctor spotted me and came over to my table. "Oh Mr. Cupp. I heard your son lived! Oh, Mr. Cupp, your son could never live." I listened quietly, captivated by his passion; fascinated by the truth. He reached over, planted his index finger on my Bible, and declared, "You *reading that book to him* made him live."

"Ohhh," he repeated while shaking his head, "He *could never* live!"

Life can be strange. Some of the most "righteous" Christians from my church never once came to the hospital to see us. Some others — who could easily be branded as non-Christian — came and brought me dinners. They sat with me and cried with me, bearing the burdens of another. These folk demonstrated the Biblical definition of true religion. I had not always been a man of deep faith. I didn't always go to church. Church was mean to me when I was a little kid. So I hadn't gone back to church since I was about fourteen or fifteen. My faith developed in my twenties when I started reading the Word a lot. And even that didn't just *happen*.

You see, I had two boys, and my sister-in-law had two boys. (Incidentally, I now have two grandsons.) While my ex-wife and I were raising our family, I had hoped for a little girl. I had always wanted a little girl. I think it had something to do with my mother dying when I was a little kid. I longed for a daughter. Finally, we were blessed with my dream-come-true. Our baby daughter was beautiful! Words cannot describe...

One morning, shortly after we brought our newborn home from the hospital, I went over to peek at her in her crib. To my horror, she was dead. My precious princess was gone. Sudden Infant Death Syndrome! It just broke our hearts. In the midst of my pain, I fixed up her room. We didn't even know what to name her. We hadn't picked out a name because we'd been surprised with a daughter. (We didn't have sonograms back then.)

There had been recent thunderstorms, and the day of her funeral was gloomy, rainy, and muddy. At twenty-two years-old, I was burying my only daughter at Babyland, and listening to a preacher who wasn't saying anything of any good. They lowered that little casket (my treasure chest) into the ground. As the mourners headed back up the hill, I looked up at the sky. There were signs that it was going to rain again; big thick, dark clouds. Great! My thoughts drifted toward God, but everything in my heart was negative. Trudging up that hill, I almost slipped in the mud. And now we could expect even more rain and more mud!

At that stage of my life, I didn't know the Bible. But as I looked up, one more time, I saw a beam of light part through the clouds. Later, people would try to tell me that it was the sun, but I know the sun was hidden behind dark, August, thunderclouds. As I looked up at that light, the light came through me. I immediately felt weak. I remember thinking, "I'm going to fall down in front of all these

people, and they're all going to think that I'm weak! I can't fall down."
I had just won my first championship boxing match. (110 guys com-
peted.) I reached for the fender of a parked car to brace myself, and
I looked around at the others and at my wife. Apparently, nobody
had noticed anything. I was amazed! "Didn't anybody see that?" I
wondered. "Didn't anybody see that light?" I'd just told God I didn't
see Him; I didn't see anything good. "Everything is bad, God," I'd
declared in my thoughts. So as I climbed into my car, I tried to pull
myself together. "What was that??"

To reach the exit, drivers had to circle back, tracing the perimeter
of the property. Halfway around (set-back from the street) was a
statue of Jesus Christ with His arms raised. Beneath, a sign quoted
John 8:12 – I AM THE LIGHT OF THE WORLD. As I took it
all in, I realized that this could be the answer to the mystery! "Was
that God?" I wondered. "Was that strange light I saw from God? I
think that was God!"

When I got home that night, I gathered some little pamphlets that
my uncle had sent me. He was a Christian, living in Pennsylvania. I read
them, and I thought, "I've been to church. I've been to Sunday School.
I've been to catechism; to confirmation; baptized; but I don't know..."

I remembered I had said a prayer when I was six years old, on the
balcony with my mother. I had asked Jesus to come into my heart; told
Him that I believed in Him. "But I don't know if that was real. Was
I serious?" Well, I knew I was gonna make it serious now. I got out of
bed, got on my knees and asked Jesus to forgive me and come into my
heart; to be my Savior.

I knew before I got up off my knees that something had happened.
I felt like a weight had been lifted from me. "As newborn babes desire
the sincere milk of the Word, that they may grow thereby..." I didn't
know any of those verses, at the time, but I remembered there was a
Bible packed away in the attic. I hunted through boxes till I found it. I
started reading it and I said, "God, I'm going to read this book. They
say this is Your book. I've heard all kinds of stuff about it –it's true;
it's mixed-up; it's this; it's that...I don't know. But they say it's Your
book, and I'm going to read it. And You're going to have to show me
it's Your book, God, or I'm going to throw it right in that trash can."

DOCTOR JESUS STILL PERFORMS MIRACLES

That's exactly what I said. I read it through, twice. I've never stopped reading it, since, because I know that it's God's Word. I knew, in my soul, that it was speaking to me. I was born again; saved!

I named my little girl Christine, without knowing what it meant. It sounded like a good name. Some days later, I wondered about it, so I looked it up. It means "God's Messenger."

I read God's word to George, night after night. Two months rolled into three. Three gave way to four. Finally, after about six months, George fully regained consciousness. At this point, he weighed about 135 pounds. He was infantile when he first woke up. He was a bit restless and child-like. He tried to talk to me, and he would tell me, "I saw them! I watched them. They were sewing up my legs" (pointing to his lower thighs). He kept trying to talk. He couldn't smile but he kept trying to talk. I would try to calm him; settle him down. "Try to relax, Son." None of us — his family — had yet seen George's bare legs, but he kept referring to them. I kept telling him, "Relax, George." But he insisted on communicating to me this consistent message, "I watched them working on my legs; putting stitches in my legs." I knew about staples, but I hadn't heard any of them talk about "stitches." He said this so often that it troubled me, so I finally asked the doctor.

A typical scientist, the doctor answered my question with a question, "Where does he say that we sewed him?"

"His legs," I said. "He keeps insisting that he watched you sew his legs."

The doctor looked me in the eye and nodded. "He's right. His legs are the only part of his body where we used sutures. The bones had so badly torn his skin that we couldn't use staples, so we stitched the superficial layers of his legs." For the millionth time that winter, my spirit was flooded with awe and wonder.

Many years later, this recollection of a mysterious awareness remained with George. While paramedics, doctors and nurses had been fighting for his life; while fluids and drugs surged through his veins; while his blood chemistry deteriorated to lethal levels of disequilibrium; while doctors barked orders, and anxious voices and alarms buzzed in his ears; while the odors of oxygen, blood, latex, plastic, antiseptics, and human beings toyed with the minutest hairs of his nostrils; while my son was clinically dead; George "saw himself" rising above the gurney, and watched them labor to save his own legs. "I remember thinking, 'That's me! I'm looking at me!' And I saw the light. I didn't just see the light; I felt the light. The light permeated me," George explained as he openly wept over the beauty of the memory. "It was the most wonderful feeling, Dad. It was like a liquid force of love."

Epilogue

When my son was leaving the hospital, Dr. Bakulesh Patel, the head surgeon, bid us farewell. "I can never forget your son," he remarked. "He could never survive."

My son was young and strong. People said (and still say) that youth and strength were in his favor and that's why he survived. But Dr. Patel spelled it out clearly, "That's like somebody taking a double-barreled shotgun and saying, 'You are young and strong — you can survive this,' and then shooting you in the chest. It would be impossible to live. Your son...it was impossible for him to live."

So I asked him the million-dollar question, as George was being discharged. "Doctor, why did you work on him for so long? You worked on him for about ten hours, without stopping, as I recall." Then Dr. Patel stood up and walked over, very close to me. He hovered over me with his arms encircling my head, forming a large horseshoe, but never touching me. "This is exactly what happened," he said. "Although I was dead-tired and ready to give up, I felt some kind of force that held me up and would not let me go!"

Soaking in his words, my soul welled up with songs of praise and gratitude to the Almighty God! It was clear to me that — whether or not he realized it — Dr. Patel was referring to the Holy Spirit of God, or an angel of God. That's right — "The angel of the Lord encampeth round about them that fear him, and delivereth them." (Psalm 34:7)

Dropping his arms at his side, Dr. Patel turned to my son, broke down in tears and declared, "I will never forget your son for as long as I live. I have no explanation for him living, except it must be that his work on earth is not finished."

The Story of
Ron Rambo

As told by Ron

Ron Rambo preaches with a passion seldom heard these days. His message, one bright morning, was on the power of prayer, which he illustrated by sharing a personal story about a time when a two-second delay would've killed him! God has given him an experience and a testimony that simply has to be told! It is a pleasure to be able to fully retell it here.

My parents got married at age sixteen, and by the time they were twenty-two, they had five children. I was number four — born in the early 1960s. We lived in Riverdale, Maryland; started school at Riverdale Elementary for two years; moved to Landover Hills and went to the elementary school there; attended Glen Ridge Junior High; and finally graduated from Bladensburg High, in Bladensburg, Maryland.

My best childhood memories are from the days when I was ten years old. Several times that year, three kids from the neighborhood invited us to come to their church. I particularly remember Bill Wiseman and Bill Maggard. My mom was really impressed by their friendliness, their enthusiasm, and their offer to pick up us kids and bring us home. The church was Landover Hills Baptist. First we enjoyed Sunday School, and then stayed for the eleven o'clock service. In the summertime, we all piled into a station wagon and headed for a cabin in the mountains. Lots of fishing and hiking. Great fun!

My mom was so impressed by those Baptist kids, she started to attend their church. I was baptized when I was thirteen, along with

Mom and my brothers and sisters. We stayed at that church for over twenty years. Dad worked hard to provide for our big family, and although he only went to church occasionally, he had a reputation for being a man of integrity and high morals. He inspired all of us to do our very best.

From the time that Mom started going to church, she prayed with us before meals and before we went to sleep at night. Her close relationship with God gave her a great supply of patience to raise five children. She worked hard to provide for everything we needed, and we always knew she was praying for us.

During my teen years, I got into boxing; playing football; all kinds of worldly activities. I didn't spend much time in church. Mom would always tell me, "Ron, you need to get back into church. You know you are the happiest when you are close to God."

It upset Mom a bit when, like most of the guys in those days, I let my hair grow long. I told her, "Mom, it can't be a sin because even Jesus had long hair." Mom conceded, "Oh well, you will save money by not going to barber shops." Little did she know that one day my long hair would save my life.

When I graduated from high school in '79, my plan was to get into law enforcement, or to join the marines. But many of my plans changed when I fell in love with a beautiful girl named Debbie. We were married when I was only nineteen, and we had our first child.

My father, Jim Rambo, and my two older brothers, Bobby and Jimmy, were carpenters. Dad became a superintendent for one of the big companies that was contracted to Metro when they were building new subways. He designed the lumber forms that were used when pouring concrete walls. After I joined the carpenters' union, attended their school, and learned to build forms, I went to work with Dad and my brothers in the subway stations.

The job was at the Metro stop at Connecticut Ave. and Elm St., N.W., in Washington, D.C. Although it was interesting work, it was often quite risky because we were always working either high up (sometimes on swinging scaffolds) or down deep in the tunnels. The tunnels were usually cold and damp, so there was always a danger of slipping and sliding. The guys that were pouring the wet concrete had to wait for us, so they were always pushing us to work faster — someone always yelling at us to hurry up!

Once, when I was only nineteen years old and still an apprentice, I was working from a swinging scaffold on the side of the entrance way. The scaffold, supported by two ropes hanging from above and secured at the ground level, was about seventy-five feet up in the air. Just coming back from lunch, I started to step onto the scaffold when one of the carpenters called out to me — something about nails. I stepped backward onto the wall so I could hear what he was saying. A split second later, a big backhoe (working at the ground level, below) accidentally hit one of the ropes that supported the scaffold. WHACK! The rope broke, and the scaffold (that I had nearly stepped onto) swung crazily up in the air, only supported by one rope. If I had not backed up when I did, I would have crashed seventy-five feet to the rocky ground below. That was just my first close call! As I look back on similar experiences, I thank God that because of Mom's prayers, God is always looking out for me.

About a month later, we were on one of the newly built platform areas, and we were working on the foundation of a wall about 100 feet below ground. This was a new building, so it was mainly just dirt, rock and tunnels. We were doing a concrete pour. We had just finished building the form, and walked about fifty feet over to the other side of the tunnel to make a form for another wall. Another crew was getting ready to pour; attaching hoses to bring the concrete down. This was a Friday afternoon, and everyone was in a hurry, hoping to get the job done early.

We had all brought our lunches with us, and were just taking a lunch break in our work areas. The carpenter who was sitting next to me asked me, "Have you ever seen a concrete form bust?"

I said , "No. I've seen concrete leaking from a smaller form, and we had to hurry to brace the form up, but I never saw one bust."

Then he asked me, "Have you ever heard one bust?"

I said, "No, have you?"

He said, "Yes! It sounds just like a shotgun blast! Listen — if you ever hear a sound like a shotgun going off, don't look up to see where the shot came from. Just turn and run away. If you look, you won't have time to get out of the way."

The wall they were pouring was about twenty feet tall. They had poured the bottom section of the wall earlier, so the part they were pouring, now, was ten feet above us. There were thirty-three cubic yards of concrete in this pour. The wall was probably a hundred feet long and twelve inches thick. The forms were constructed out of plywood, 2 x 4s and 2 x 6s bolted together. They were very sturdy and we seldom had any complications, but there was plenty of pressure for the forms to sustain.

They were setting up for the pour. They started pouring about 2:30 p.m.; by 3:05 p.m., they had finished. They had poured about three and a half truckloads of wet concrete. When my father heard about that, he said, "No way! They poured too fast!" My father said, "Get everybody out of there. They're going to lose that form. They poured too fast!" Unfortunately, my dad was not in my work area, and not within earshot.

We were packing up to go when my foreman called and said, "Rambo, we got a leak over here in this corner. Grab your wrench and hammer and get over here." I climbed a little stepladder because we had to reach up about eight feet over our heads to tighten the bolts, since wet concrete was seeping out the bottom. We thought we had it under control. "That's all we'll be able to do. I think we're good," my foreman commented.

I turned around to get my toolbox. My back was to the pour. The foreman had walked off to the side. He had just stepped out, but I was headed in the opposite direction. I had taken about two steps when... BOOM!! It sounded like a shotgun blast. It was instantaneous — no time to think! Remembering what my friend had told me earlier, I jumped and landed in the gulley. As I was flying through the air, I instinctively grabbed my knees and doubled up like a ball in order to protect my limbs. A huge 4 x 6 lumber board hit me in the back and pinned me to the ground. In a few seconds, I was buried in wet concrete about three feet deep!

The next thing I recall, someone was grabbing my hair and pulling my head out of the concrete. Bobby Rawlings, one of the carpenters, had seen where I went down. He couldn't see me because I was covered with concrete, but thank God, he saw where I went down and he reached in and found my head. (If my hair had been as short as it is now, I would have been history!) When he pulled me out, first he cleared my airway, my mouth and my eyes. At that time, he was the only one there. He pulled me by the arms, dislocating both shoulders. He was just a young guy and didn't know what to do.

My father, who had been in the carpenter shop on the upper level, heard the bang and rushed down to the lower level. My two brothers also came running. My father shouted, "Get me a water hose!" First they washed my face off, then Dad said, "Don't pull on his arms anymore. We'll have to dig him out in a hurry before the concrete hardens." So they started digging with shovels. Dad kept shouting, "Watch his legs." Several guys, including my two brothers, worked with a fast and furious determination to get me out.

First, they got the timber off my back. Then, racing against time, they carefully dug out the concrete all around me. They lifted and carried me on a stretcher to the one-man elevator. An ambulance rushed me to Suburban Hospital in Bethesda. The date was Friday, August 8, 1980.

When the doctor came in, he said, "When I first saw you, I couldn't understand how you ever made it out of there alive! It's amazing that you weren't injured far worse."

I was in the hospital for two weeks. There were three compression injuries to my spine. No broken bones! But, since then, I've had five surgeries on my shoulders.

When I look back on it, I realize that God warned me just in time to save my life! If my friend had not told me that story, as we ate lunch together, I'm sure my reaction would have been to turn and look up to see where the explosive sound came from. That two-second delay would have been all the devil needed to stop another Christian from being a strong witness for the Lord Jesus!

Thanks a million for your prayers, Mom!

Epilogue

At age twenty-five, I started meeting up with three dedicated Christians who were Seventh-day Adventists — Andy and Cheri Gates, and Ramona. We began to seriously study the Bible together, and in time, I was convinced that the Adventist faith was right for me. I now serve as an elder in the Seventh-day Adventist Church in Prince Frederick, Maryland.

I'm so happy that my oldest son, Ron, Jr., has already preached his first sermon. Praise the Lord Jesus!

The Story of
Joe Hamilton

As told by Joe

My parents and my five siblings and I lived in College Park, Maryland until I was eleven years old. I attended Holy Redeemer Elementary until the fifth grade. Then, we moved to Calvert County in Southern Maryland, where I attended Our Lady Star of the Sea from the sixth to tenth grade. Since there were only seven kids in the high school during my sophomore year, they closed the school and so, beginning in the eleventh grade, I attended Calvert Senior High in Prince Frederick, and graduated from there.

My experience in the U.S. Navy equipped me to get a job in construction electrical work. For thirty years, I worked in civil service as an electrical equipment repairer at Patuxent Naval Air Base in Maryland.

When I was 27 years old, I met a charismatic prayer group and, to me, their way of praying made God seem very real. I was pious enough and religious enough, but God wasn't as personal to me as He was to those people, so I challenged God. I said, "Are You really real?" That was my question, and I went through all the usual answers like, "Look at the beauty of the earth and all the creation." That didn't work. I wanted something more tangible, like I'm talking to an individual who is sitting right there in front of me. So finally (when push came to shove), I asked for this "baptism in the Holy Spirit" that they talked about.

They responded, "Did you take The Life and the Spirit seminar?" No. The seminar had just closed. I would have to wait another month or two. I said, "Aw, forget it." My doubts all rushed forward again.

One day, it was like God grabbed me by the shoulders and said, "Joe Hamilton, what must I do to prove to you that I am real?" I answered,

"Well, I'll tell You. You want me to obey the Ten Commandments. And You want me to believe that You are really real, that there is a heaven, and there is a hell. I don't want to go to hell, but the truth is — I don't want to follow Your leadings, nor Your Ten Commandments. I want to do my thing. So, it doesn't make sense for You to create me to go to hell. Therefore, You do in me whatever it is I need...to get to heaven when I die."

So this is what God did: He gave me such a love for the person of Jesus Christ! I've known all about the Blessed Trinity. I've known all about that, but I've never met the Lord personally. Now I am so wonderfully in love with Him. I'm head over heels. That was January 31, 1976, seven o'clock in the morning. I woke up just infatuated with Jesus. Out of this, I also experienced the gift of the Holy Spirit, but that was much later.

The following Memorial Day weekend, I attended a conference at Notre Dame University in Indiana. The theme was, "Lord, the Kingdom, the Power, and the Glory are Yours." So I went to the Glory workshop and they talked about letting the Holy Spirit use you, go ahead and touch you, and so forth. But I had always been afraid because when I was about twelve years old, my brother told me this story: There was a person praying before the crucifix, the statue came off the crucifix, and Jesus was present to him. That experience was so wonderful that the guy had to die. He couldn't live on earth any more. He had to go to heaven. Well, twelve years old what can I say? Now these people were saying, "Let God touch you. Let God give you a language to pray in," and all those kinds of things. Well, I gave in, and I'm so glad I did. Because of that touch, God was able to move into my person through inner healing; through the healing of memories; through a deep abiding love; and instilling in me a confidence that I could not possibly have gotten from other people. I needed a deep love that was unconditional, and this can only come through the Lord Jesus by His Holy Spirit.

Eventually, years later, I got to the point where Jesus took me "home" and introduced me to my Father — my real Father. He helped me let go of my natural father, saying, "This is your real Father." Life as a Christian is a very wholesome, healthy experience.

Through that, I think the Lord just gave me a gift of praise. I love to praise God. Not just, "Oh God, I praise You because You created the world and this big mountain," and whatever...or, "I praise You because You did this for me and that for me."

Oh no!

"I praise You just because You are God and there is no other."

In this praise, I have experienced three major miracles. The skeptic will always have something to say, but why would I ever want to take away glory from the Lord? The first miracle was that the Lord healed my celiac disease. Celiac disease is a genetic disease. It's usually in Scandinavia, British or Mediterranean areas. Many people have it. It is an autoimmune disease that destroys the villi in your intestines, and when you eat something that has gluten in it, you cannot digest the food. Gluten is found in wheat, barley and rye, and because of cross-contamination (where oats are grown) oats also have gluten. In the United States, you stay away from all four of those foods. My sister found out about it through much research (over a decade) because no one we knew could tell us anything about it. These days, people are learning that when you are going to the bathroom all the time, it may be because you are eating gluten.

In the year 2000, I got my first colonoscopy and they found a tumor. So they were going to operate, and my sister said, "Please stop eating gluten because that is going to irritate the intestines (just in case you do have celiac disease). We will find out later. Right now, we don't know if you do because they would have to do an endoscopy and take a sample from your intestines to find out if you have that disease. It is very invasive and very hard to do." So I agreed, "Okay, I will stop eating gluten."

Just one week after the colonoscopy, they had me on the operating table, taking out nine inches of my colon. Everything was fine. I didn't have to do radiation or chemo, or anything like that. They felt very confident that I was going to be okay. Well, I was...for about five years.

In June 2002, my wife Eileen and I went to a symposium on healing in Minneapolis, Minnesota. On the panel, there were five or six people who served in the healing ministry, and the audience could ask them all kinds of questions. During my prayer time, while we were there, I felt like the Lord was telling me, "I'm going to heal your celiac disease."

I thought, *Okay. I'm sure that's me talking, more than it is Jesus.* But I said, *Okay, Lord, that will be nice. Call me later.*

The following January, Eileen and I attended a charismatic retreat in Emmitsburg, western Maryland. While we were there, an evangelist visited us, and he encouraged us by saying, "You have just celebrated Jesus in your midst and you need to apply that to your life. Don't just let it be a religious ritual. Let Jesus be real. Since He is here, ask Him whatever you want — just like they did back in Jerusalem. Do it now. This is why Jesus is present to us and He left us this holy communion." So, this is exactly what we did.

The first thing that popped-up in my mind was to ask Jesus to heal my celiac disease. I thought, *You know what — I'm going to, this time.* I had peace about it, and I was not the least bit anxious. I thought, *Lord, I give it to You. Let Thy will be done.*

There were three lines for healing. I decided not to get in line for the evangelist, who is known for the gift of healing. Neither would I go to the Retreat Master. That's what everybody does because he is anointed for healing. It occurred to me to go to these two ladies who looked just like "anybody." They were just like me. So I went over to them and said, "I need a gene change. I know it's an unusual request, but I have celiac disease and I feel like the Lord wants to heal me. It's an inherited disease. You don't catch this from anyone. It's inherited, so I need a gene change."

They said, " Okay. That's fine." I could have been asking for a drink of water. They didn't care. Well, why should they care? They're not the ones healing, anyway. The Lord is. So they said, "Oh Lord, please bless Joe. Take care of whatever he needs." It was a very simple prayer. "Just change his genes to whatever he needs, so that he no longer has this disease. We pray in the name of Jesus. Amen."

OOOOH!

Down I went. I fell down — just resting in the Spirit like I had never done before. I had done this numerous times, but never like this! While I was on the floor, I could feel every body cell tingling! It was actually like my genes were changing all over my body from the top of my head to the bottom of my feet. It was just a tingling that was going on, and I was just so relaxed and just resting in the love of God.

People were leaving. I thought, I've got to get up. I tried to get up but I could not move! I've never had that happen. So after about five or ten minutes, I struggled to get up, and the best I could do was get to a chair. I plopped in the chair and I just stayed there thinking, God is not finished yet. So I stayed there for about a half hour. Everybody else (except my two best friends and my wife) had gone. It was marvelous! I knew God had just healed me!

I did not immediately go back to eating gluten products because wheat is very harsh on the body, and if you have not eaten wheat for a long time, even without celiac disease, it's going to be rough on you. You will be going to the bathroom a lot, and all this other stuff. You have to take it easy.

Well, here is what happened next: My wife was feeling tired, so we went to the doctor. He took a blood sample and found out that she had elevated liver enzymes, and he ordered an MRI. The nurse at the imaging center came out and said to Eileen, "You need to go see your doctor."

We said, "Okay. We'll set up an appointment."

She said, "No, you need to see him now!"

We went to the doctor, immediately. It was after-hours, but the doctor was still at his office. He said, "I haven't heard anything from the people at MRI, so I'll call them now." They reported that over 80% of her liver was covered with cancer. They said there was nothing they could do! Three weeks later, my dear wife was gone! Eileen died in March of 2003.

I had just been healed of celiac disease, but now, I surely didn't feel like celebrating. I missed Eileen terribly! She was so much a part of my life. I began to question God: What happened, Lord? Did You forget? Or maybe You just don't care. Yes, I know Your ways are higher than ours, but an old song, *I'll Never Smile Again Until I Smile at You* kept playing in my mind. I should thank God that the next time I see Eileen she will have a brand new, perfect body, but in the mean time, I didn't feel like tootin' my little horn about being cured of celiac. First, I just needed time to mourn.

The following August, I went to visit my brother-in-law and he told me, "You are probably going to wind-up in a position where you will have to eat food that contains gluten and nothing bad will happen. That will tell you that God really did heal you." Sure enough, the following November, there was another conference in Tennessee. A group of us drove down, and we spent the night in a hotel. I had my suitcase full of gluten-free food, cereals, etc. Wouldn't you know — I left the suitcase at the hotel, and didn't realize it until we arrived in Tennessee! Now I had to eat gluten. So I ate gluten and I had no problem! That's right. I never had a problem.

Still, I wanted to get more positive proof that I didn't have celiac disease, so I had an endoscopy done. The doctor said, "The biopsy did not take well. There is some redness there, so maybe…" this and that. It wasn't clear-cut. Now I got really angry with the Lord. I said, "You duped me. You said You were going to heal me, but now they tell me that possibly I still have celiac disease!"

The telephone rings. I'm there crying my eyes out. I'm just so livid! I don't know what to do with myself. It's like God is teasing me. I wanted something clear-cut, and I didn't get it. I picked up the phone and heard a voice (which I did not recognize) say to me, "You're missing the point! You're missing the point!" That was all. Then he hung up. There was some noise in the background that I could't identify. But it didn't matter. The point was that I was missing the point from God.

I was focusing on what I thought was supposed to happen. God doesn't need me to tell Him what's supposed to happen. God needs my attention! God needs my trust! God needs me to walk with Him! Don't tell God what He is supposed to do! Please do not tell God what He's got to do.

So I got the point. I let it go because the message was *Do not look for healing.* Do not look for this, that, or the other miracle. Do not look to glorify Joe. That's what would have happened. Joe would have been glorified, and Joe would have advertised, "Look what God did for Joe!" Then Joe gets all puffed up. That's the problem. Ego! Self wants to be noticed. God does this great miracle, and self wants to take glory away from God. No! I don't think so! Sure, I was going to give credit to God, but I also wanted to make sure that they came to Joe in order for God to be glorified. So God is second to Joe, in such a case. This is where I was coming from, and this is what God was healing me of.

I would never have guessed that my story would end up in a book! Now God is getting the glory because of what I went through, and I'm making sure that Joe has learned his lesson. You do not look at the healing, or the miracle, or the gift. You just look at God, and have a nice day. Period.

I fell in love again in August of 2004, and married Sally, my current wife. She knew my history. In 2000, four years earlier, I'd had cancer, but that didn't phase her. She was looking at the person, not the possible "what-ifs", which was honorable on her part. And for me, it was a blessing.

In October of 2006, I was preparing to go to Ocean City, Maryland for a surf fishing tournament, as I had done every year. I was doing exercises to help build up my stamina when I got a terrible pain in my abdomen. I went to my family doctor, Dr. Charles Bennett, who said, "I don't think you have pancreatitis. You probably just strained your muscles. Nevertheless, because of your history — you did have colon cancer before — so let's take a look."

I took a blood test, and the liver enzymes were way up. Then an MRI showed that most of my liver was covered with cancer. I would not be able to see my oncologist for a week, so Dr. Bennett told me to go fishing, anyway. Since they were not able to do surgery for a week, I went fishing. When I went to my oncologist, Dr. Arati Patel, she ordered a biopsy. Colon cancer cells had spread to my liver!

She said, "There is a new drug on the market which has been very successful. You are at fourth-stage cancer, so I will give you the heaviest dose of chemo that I can possibly give to a body of your size."

I just said, "Okay. That's fine." It was like I didn't even hear fourth stage cancer, let alone what that meant. When Eileen had been diagnosed with fourth stage cancer, it was like the Lord just closed my ears to the difficulty. It just didn't register. But my diagnosis registered with Sally, my wife. She knew fourth-stage is the last stage!

I started on the chemo. They inserted a port so they could give me the chemo intravenously. I had to take home a device that would give me an IV infusion over 24 hours. The following day, I would return to the hospital and they would disconnect it. Then I would be good for a week. Then I would go back for the same treatment for a week, and so on for three more sessions — eight weeks of chemotherapy. Finally the doctor said, "I think you need a rest. Go do something fun. Don't think about this. Don't worry about anything. Just get away and get a complete rest."

So we took off for Branson, Missouri. Chemo usually weakens you, but I was strong enough to go. One of the amazing things was that I did not lose any hair. The doctor had said, "I have never seen anyone take as much chemo as you have and not lose hair."

We came back in April and she said, "I'd like to give you another dose before we do anything because you still have large areas of cancer. I would like to reduce the disease as best we can." She explained the reason they couldn't do radiation was because the cancer was too scattered all over the liver, and radiation only works when they can get to an exact spot. So I agreed — another eight weeks of chemo.

During this time, another miracle took place: I never got sick! People taking chemotherapy usually get very nauseated, constipated, and so forth. There were times that I was either constipated or I had the runs. It was one or the other. It was hard to get that stabilized. I also had some medicine to help calm the stomach to avoid vomiting, but usually I didn't even need that. The Lord was just carrying me through this whole thing. I just want to thank the Lord for that.

It was now July of 2007, and it was time for me to get an operation. I went to Georgetown University because Dr. Patel had said, "I want you to contact Lynt B. Johnson. He's the one. If they give you anyone else, say 'No.' I used to work with him and he is very good! He is the head of the Oncology Department at Georgetown, a real wheel there, and he is a super nice gentleman."

Doctor Johnson spoke with me about the plan. It looked like about 40% of the liver would need to be removed, and since the gall bladder was situated right underneath the liver, they would remove that also.

After the operation, which took over three hours, Sally told me, "When the doctor came out, he was drenched and beat!" He felt like it was a success, but they took 50% of the liver because, during surgery, they found two more tumors that they hadn't known about. One of them was wrapped around the blood vessel which was the primary vessel providing blood to the liver. If you cut that, you're dead!

All was well. Other than a lung which collapsed temporarily during the surgery, I had no complications.

I gotta tell you, this really happened: While I was there, lying in the hospital, I just felt like I wanted to praise God; just love Him with all my might. I told God how wonderful, how awesome He is. I tell you, I had a wonderful praise meeting all by myself. That's the way God carried me through the whole thing. Cancer is depressing. Everyone knows it is depressing. But I had no depression! I had times when I was just exhausted, but that's all. I was blessed to have the right people with me at the right time. They worked with me the way I needed it.

Although I lost half my liver, it had no adverse effect on me. I went back to eating the way I normally did — glutens and all! I never lost my hair. I had a friend who said, "If you lose your hair, I'm going to cut all my hair off and be with you." I told that to my doctor. She laughed and said, "God must not want to see him bald." My hair, now, is shorter and thinner, but I never lost it.

So that was my second biggest miracle — how I survived fourth stage cancer.

Four months later in November, 2007, God blessed me with a third miracle. I was well enough to go on a two-week car trip with Sally and her parents. We went to Wisconsin, then to Canada, where we enjoyed much sightseeing. I was only two months out of the hospital.

One night I had felt this kind of clammy feeling, a little dizzy, etc., but it passed. I just thought it was from a little indigestion, or something. The next day, I picked up a forty-pound bag of water-softening salt, and I got this clammy feeling. I recalled when I worked in civil service as an electrician, we had to take CPR courses, and I knew about heart attacks and what to look for, according to the films. Well, forget those films! My symptoms were nothing like that, at all. I didn't feel pressure on my chest, or a numbness in my arm, or anything like that. I just felt tired, and had a cold, sweaty kind of feeling. My gums on the lower jaw were aching terribly! Really sore! No one had ever told me anything like that was related to a heart attack. So I lay down, and Sally called 911. Not only was I having a heart attack, but when they hooked me to the EKG on the way to the hospital, my heart rhythm changed for the worse! When I got to the hospital and had calmed down, they called the helicopter and transferred me by MedEvac to Washington Hospital Center. I learned later that if I had remained in the condition that I was in during the ambulance ride, I would have possibly just died. But thank God, I had calmed down. My heart was beating regularly, and there was enough blood pressure that I was okay. I was well enough to go in the helicopter.

Again, the Lord carried me through. I wasn't concerned at all. While I was in the helicopter, the rescuer said, "Would you like to look out the window?"

"Sure! I would like that." She propped me up a bit so I could look out the window. It was great! The trees were beautiful in their autumn colors. We flew over Andrews Air Force Base, and I enjoyed seeing Washington, D.C., by air. In spite of the heart attack, I enjoyed the ride.

When we arrived at Washington Hospital Center, they immediately ran some tests to determine what the problem was. They found five blockages, so I needed a quintuple bypass. They said if I had been taking chemo at the time, the treatment plan would have been different. Maybe they would've just let me go! Again, I can only praise the Lord!

The very next day I was on the operating table, which was a blessing, because often one has to wait in line. They actually removed the heart from my body to work on it. First, they harvested one vein, but it didn't work, so they had to take out another vein. All very complicated. Anyhow, when they finished their magic, they stuck my heart back in me. And here I am!

There were no post-operative complications. All the praise goes to God. His consolation kept me from being concerned. I tell people, "Don't wait and try to bargain with God if you have a problem. Don't wait till the last minute to get to know Him and say, "Oh God, if you get me through this, I'll be a good boy for the rest of my life." Don't try it because you don't even think about God when you are on a gurney. You don't even think about God when you are lying on the stretcher having a heart attack. You don't think about God when the doctor says you've got 40% of your liver covered in cancer (and your wife died not too long ago from the same disease). You just don't think about God. So what did I think about? I was just blank. Just numb. The thing is that God was consoling me, already. I had the love of God already, so I just trusted Him to bring me through.

When you've been baptized by the Holy Spirit, there's always a presence of God within you, no matter what is going on. You nurture that through constantly praising God and asking God for the grace to love Him more, each day. Then when things do happen, you just walk through it.

Jesus just spoke truth to the people, and they got mad at Him. They were going to pick up stones and throw them at Him, and so forth, and He just walked right through. It's that kind of presence that the baptism of the Holy Spirit gives a person during these traumatic occasions…a presence of peace that just "walks right through."

God has indeed changed me. I truly enjoy life every day, walking with Jesus, following His Ten Commandments, and loving my neighbor as myself!

The Story of
Chris Brown

As told by Chris

I have always hated to wear glasses. When I was a teenager, I thought they made me look like a sissy, and not very attractive to girls. So when I was eighteen years old, I got contact lenses. It worked! The next time I asked a girl for a date, she said yes.

Unfortunately, my association with girls in the neighborhood got me involved with some other guys who were not so good for me. I guess, up to that point, I had kept pretty close to home. My parents were devout Christians, and they never let me get very far out of their sight. However, like most teens, I had all the answers, and I wanted to fit in with the popular crowd. Then, when I got a car, picking up girls was easy. My girlfriends had expensive taste, and before I wised-up, I was deep into debt!

My girlfriend's father, a captain in the Navy, was pretty cool. He knew I was heading for big trouble, so he gave me some good advice. He said, "Chris, the best thing you can do is to join the Navy. It's a good life and it will give you a fresh beginning. You can pay off your debts, save some money, and later, with the GI Bill, you can get a better education." Of course, he was probably thinking, at the same time, I would be getting away from his daughter...and I couldn't blame him for that. I took his advice. On September 9, 1992, I signed up for the Navy. I was eighteen years old.

After three months in boot camp, I was stationed aboard the USS PYRO, a World War II ammunition ship. My duties involved taking care of the life boats and helping to train some deep-sea divers. I really enjoyed life at sea. It was clean, healthy, and I especially enjoyed seeing the beautiful sunsets — watching that ball of fire sink into the Pacific Ocean.

And I thanked God for freeing me from that crazy lifestyle that had nearly trapped me.

We were doing some training maneuvers near a small naval base on an island in the Pacific, which was close to San Francisco. Occasionally, our ship tied up at the island to take on supplies. About the only thing on the island was a small Navy hospital and a landing field for small aircraft.

One day, some of the guys and I decided to go ashore on the weekend and try to hook-up with some of those pretty nurses stationed at the hospital. I put my contacts in, which I had not worn at all during three months in boot camp. Then three other sailors and I hit the beach and started to walk toward the hospital.

As the day wore on, I kept feeling that something was happening with the contacts. My eyes became dry, itchy and very uncomfortable. I saw the medical corpsman on duty. She said, "The only thing I can give you now are these eye drops. Use these drops as needed. It should help relieve your discomfort. They are very strong, so only use them as needed." I used the eye drops and immediately began to feel better. But a couple hours later, my eyes began to bother me again, so I used more drops, and more drops and more drops.

Suddenly, things began to appear darker and darker, until I couldn't see at all! I learned, later, the lenses had begun to deteriorate!

One of my friends helped me get back to the ship, and he took me up to sick bay. The chief corpsman asked me, "What were you using?" I showed him the eye drops, and he said, "I don't believe this. Who gave these to you?" I told him, and he said, "These eye drops are for chemical biological warfare. If there was a poisonous agent in the air, you would use these to flush the eyes out. But now, using these drops, you have paralyzed the muscles in your eyes to stay open. You have been absorbing the sunlight in its fullness all this time, and your eyes are severely dry. You have damaged your eyes." That's all he said, but the tone of his voice told me that it was probably much worse than he described.

They bandaged me to keep the light out of my eyes, and took me back to the hospital. The doctors on duty had no idea how to treat me.

They simply put a heavy bandage across my face to block the light, and assigned me to a bed for the night. They planned to send me to San Francisco the next day where, hopefully, I could get some help.

I must admit, I began to panic inwardly. The thought of being permanently blind was scary! I asked a nurse to dial for me, and I talked to my parents who were living in Prince Frederick, Maryland. Dad answered the phone. I said, "Dad, I'm going blind." Dad asked Mom and my brother to pick up the extension and I briefly told them what happened. Then I said, "I wish I could come home."

Dad said, "Oh, Son, I wish we could come get you, but you're under contract with the Navy. One thing we can do, Chris — we can pray for you. We know the Lord can heal you." My family prayed fervently over the phone. Later, Dad told me they all knelt together on the kitchen floor and prayed some more.

I tried to sleep, but I feared my faith was not as strong as my folks' faith. I could not help but imagine what life would be like without my eyesight. I know seeing-eye dogs are quite wonderful, but could a dog read a menu to me? Could a dog describe a sunset? What kind of girl would marry a blind man?

It seemed like I just tossed and turned for hours before finally dozing off around midnight. The next thing I knew, I felt someone removing my bandage, and I heard a voice say, "Hey, what's going on here? Why are you removing the bandage? Who are you?" (He sounded like the doctor who had bandaged me.) The nurse quickly interjected, "Sir, this is Lieutenant Commander Morgan. He is an ophthalmologist." Then I heard another voice. "Good evening, Sir. I was on my way to Portland when my plane had engine problems and we were forced to land here, tonight. Since the mechanics are working on the plane, I decided to tour the hospital. When I saw this man in bandages, I asked what was wrong with him. She (he must have pointed to the nurse) told me the story, and gave me permission to examine him. I trust that this is okay with you, sir?"

"Absolutely!" the staff doctor answered. "We don't know how to treat this man. Hopefully, we can send him to the hospital in Frisco tomorrow, but please examine him and see what you think."

Dr. Morgan continued removing the bandage. Finally, he said, "I have dealt with this type of injury before, and I can tell you — unless

DOCTOR JESUS STILL PERFORMS MIRACLES

this man gets treated right away, he will be permanently blind! With your permission and your assistance, we can do it now."

The nurse helped me get on a gurney, and they quickly wheeled me into the operating room. Dr. Morgan said to me, "We need to sedate you so you will not feel any pain."

When I woke up the next morning, Dr. Morgan was gone. He had removed and discarded the contact lenses and left instructions with the nurse and hospital staff. I was told, "The procedure was successful. Keep this bandage on for three days to block all light. The fourth day, you can remove it, but always wear sunglasses when you are in bright sunlight."

I telephoned home again to tell them their prayers were answered, and my eyes would be okay. Dad shouted, "Hallelujah!" a few times, and Mom was laughing and crying with joy she didn't have words to express.

Epilogue

About three weeks later, our ship tied up again at that same island, so I went ashore to visit the nurse and express my gratitude for her care. It was the first time I had actually seen her. Then I went to the cafeteria, got a cup of coffee and sat down to read a newspaper. After awhile, an officer approached me. "Are you Chris Brown?" he asked.

"Yes sir," I answered, "and who are you?"

"I am Lieutenant Commander Morgan, the doctor who treated your eyes," he replied.

I jumped out of my chair, began pumping his hand and thanking him profusely. "How can I ever thank you, enough?"

"Well, Chris, you need to thank God. He did it all. I'm sure you heard that my plane's engine started to miss as we were flying over, and we were forced to land. Two mechanics worked on my plane for about five hours. Now let me tell you the rest of the story.

"When I went back to the plane and asked the mechanics what the problem was, they said, 'Sir, we could not find one thing wrong with your engine. It's in top condition.'

"Chris, somebody was praying. Just thank God that I was the right man, at the right place, at the right time."

This just demonstrates that the things I learned as a kid in Sunday School are true! God is omniscient, omnipotent, and omnipresent!

I have drawn closer to the Lord the last two years. I have a lovely wife, three beautiful children, a good job at the post office in Lima, Ohio — and I never wear contact lenses.

The Story of
Bobby Mammen
As told by Bobby and her husband, Jacob

I was born in Adoor, Kerala, India in the mid 1970s. We had a very luxurious and colorful life. I went to Sunday school and worshipped Mary and the Catholic Saints until I was in the fifth grade. About that time, my father, P. M. Thomas, converted to Seventh-day Adventism. After completing his studies in religion from an Adventist college in Pune, Maharashtra, he became a pastor in the Adventist church in a village in Kerala, and he began to teach the Bible to my mother, my brother and me.

I studied in public school up to the seventh grade. We then moved to a town where I completed high school at Saint George Catholic School. At age 18, I went to Pune Maharashtra to study nursing.

I married Jacob in 1998, and in 2001, we had our first baby — a boy named Neil. At that time I had a Bachelor of Science degree in Nursing. We moved to Laurel, Maryland in the USA, in December, 2002. About six months later, I found a job as a caregiver at Arden Courts, a nursing home. I worked there until our second baby — a beautiful girl named Neha — was born in October of 2005.

Naturally I missed my friends in India, so at times I felt lonely and began to read the Bible more often and became closer to the Lord. Every day when Jacob went to work, I was home by myself and had a chance to read a lot more. My father gave me an Indian Bible, so I always read from that. It's written in the Malayalam language. Even though I read and prayed a lot, I didn't have much understanding of the Bible. I collected several videos of Bible stories: Joseph, David, and all the Bible heroes whom I greatly enjoyed watching!

Some time after my second baby was born, I began to have swelling in my hands and joints. At that time, I did not have a lot of pain. I didn't know what was happening until I took my husband to our family doctor, Tony Kannarkat, for a physical examination. He noticed my hands and thought that it was arthritis, but he wasn't sure. So he referred me to a specialist. For the next four years, I suffered with symptoms of chronic arthritis. Since the special injectable medicines are very expensive, the insurance company made sure I had explored other treatment options. The doctor tried different medicines like methotrexate, prednisone, etc. They didn't work. Then they started special injectable medicines like Humira, Remicade, and Simponi. These injections worked only for the first six months. In addition, they had warned me that I would not be able to have more children if I started the injections, so I agreed to make the sacrifices.

I was always crying to the Lord, "Why me? Why me?" One day when I was watching TV, there was a man holding a Bible, and I felt like he was speaking directly to me. "Do you think that you have prayed for something for a long time and the Lord has not heard you?" Then he said, "Open John, chapter 15, verse 7, and read it. Jesus said, 'If ye abide in Me, and My words abide in you, you shall ask what ye will, and it shall be done unto you.' I cried that day because the text was true! I started praying and fasting more often, and began reading more of God's words.

Meanwhile, a prayer group at my church (Bell Branch Adventist Church) especially prayed for me. Also, my sister-in-law, Serin, introduced me to Pastor Rajendran, who lives in India. Although we had never met, he used to pray for me on the telephone. He and his church prayed for me consistently. Through all the prayers, I felt much better for a time, but again the pain started...and for three weeks, the pain was so severe I could not get out of bed! My whole body was very sensitive. I could not even touch my clothes! I would scream and cry. Jacob would have to carry me to the bathroom. I thank God for my two children, Neil and Neha, who brought me food and helped me in so many ways.

Then we phoned my pastor, Ken Coleman, at Bell Branch Seventh-day Adventist Church in Gambrills, Maryland, and asked him for prayer. He said, "I can pray for you, but I can't share your pain." What a compassionate thing to say! He came to my home and prayed for me, but there was no change. I was so disappointed.

One day I called Pastor Rajendran in India. He said, "We feel that you need to call your pastor and ask him to come to your home with elders from your church, lay hands on you, anoint you with oil and pray for you, according to James, chapter 5, in the Bible." That very same day, Don Richardson, an elder in my church, spoke nearly the same words: "You should ask the pastor to come with elders from the church, lay hands on you, anoint you with oil and pray for you." So Jacob called Pastor Coleman and he was happy to come the next day. He came along with four elders from the church (including, Rick Layton, Don Richardson, Linda Fredland, and Robin Oldfather) while others stayed at the church and prayed. Pastor Coleman brought a small bottle of olive oil. He put a drop of oil on his finger and placed it on my forehead. Then they all laid hands on me and prayed. They left immediately, but Jacob, Mother, and I continued to pray for another hour.

After the prayer, I felt calm, and the next day I could get up and do things. Usually my husband is the one who is holding me up in the morning, and it takes up to ten o'clock before I can move. After they prayed for me, I got up by myself. My mother was making tea for me, so she thought she needed to bring it upstairs to me, but then I came down. She was amazed to see me moving around and doing housework. She looked at me as if she was seeing a miracle walking, and she shed tears that only a mother can shed. That was December 11, 2010.

Everyone who worked in Jacob's office had met me and knew about my situation. Many of them had visited us at home and had been praying, as well. The next day, December 12th, I showed up at Jacob's office. When everyone came out to see me, they found me clapping my hands and jumping up in the air! I did. I did! Needless to say, my mother was not the only one crying.

I never went back to being bedridden. Occasionally, if I am very tired, I may have a little pain and swelling in the mornings. Whenever I do, I pray. Now I know how God takes care of me. From reading James 5:15 and 16, I know that when I do something wrong, I must confess my sin to the Lord, and pray for forgiveness. My pastor would always say to me, read Isaiah 55:6, "Seek ye the Lord while He may be found.

Call upon Him while He is near." That is true. That is very true. Take time to pray every day because you never know when God's Spirit is "near" to you. Do not be too tired to pray.

I've always been a shy person, but no more! For the next three Sabbaths, I stood up in my church and praised the Lord for my healing. If you tell me to stand in the middle of the road and shout praise to the Lord, I will do it!

None of the medicine that doctors had given me (for four years) had done a bit of good. But after this time of prayer, the doctor changed my medicine, and now it works! My specialist said, "Bobby, I cannot believe you...you look so different!" So praise the Lord! I told the doctor what happened. I tell everybody what happened.

Epilogue

Two days after my healing, my previous supervisor at Arden Courts called me. She told me about a job opportunity at a nursing facility in Potomac. I went to work there as Director of Nursing, and in eighteen months I was promoted to Executive Director. God is so good!

I pray my story will be a blessing to many!

The Story of
Zachary Kinney, Jr.
As told by Zachary and his mother, Wanda

WANDA: I had a sick feeling all day — like a premonition. I didn't know why, but I felt very troubled in my spirit. Then about 10 p.m., Steve asked Zach to give him a ride to Bladensburg, where Steve would meet his girlfriend who would be just getting off work. Steve was a kid who used to hang out in our neighborhood, even though he wasn't local to Oxon Hill. There was something about Steve that I didn't trust. Maybe it was because he never looked me in the eye when talking to me.

Zach was thirty-one years old, living here at home, and sometimes lacked good judgment. I told Zach, "You know, Son, nothing good happens after dark. I wish you wouldn't go out this late. Please just tell Steve you're sorry, but it's too late. He's just a kid — not dry behind the ears yet. He oughta be home in bed this time of night! Wise up, Son. You know if something happens to him, you'll get the blame."

ZACHARY: I love Mom, but sometimes she worries too much. I'd had promised Steve I'd take him over there, and I didn't want to go back on my word. Besides, he'd given me five dollars for gas money, so it would've been hard to let him down.

WANDA: Just as I feared, about two o'clock in the morning, a knock on my door woke me up. Two county policemen asked me, "Do you have a son about fifteen years old?"

I said, "No sir. My son is thirty-one years old. Oh no! Please tell me, what's going on? Why do you ask?"

"We arrested a young guy (about fifteen years old) who was speeding on the Baltimore-Washington Parkway...heading towards Baltimore. The registration card in the glove department says the car belongs to you."

"Where is my son?" I cried.

"Sorry, Ma'am. That's all we can tell you," they said. They gave me the keys to Zach's Jeep, and left me standing there.

I had barely fallen asleep (about five a.m.), when the phone rang. "Hello. May I speak to Mrs. Kinney?"

"Yes. This is Mrs. Kinney."

"I'm calling from Prince Georges General Hospital. I'm so sorry to tell you, Mrs. Kinney, your son, Zachary, was brought here this morning to the Intensive Care Unit."

"Dear God!" my soul prayed. "What happened to him?"

"He has been shot. It's pretty serious. We've transferred him to the University of Maryland Shock Trauma Hospital in Baltimore. You'd better go to the hospital, right away. He may not survive."

I called my brother (William) and my two sisters (Terry and Pam) and we all jumped in the car. My husband (Zachary, Sr.) bravely drove us to the hospital. I kept telling him to go faster.

I'll never forget the date — February 25, 2008. When we arrived at 6:30 a.m., several doctors were working on him, so we had to wait. Some nurse asked me if Zachary had a last will and testament. "The doctors do not believe he will survive...and they said, 'If he does live,' he'll probably be a vegetable." Eventually, it was suggested to us that we let them pull the plug.

I was horrified! "No! No! No! Don't say that! Don't even think about pullin' no plug! We serve the Almighty God Jehovah...and He is able to save him to the utmost! Things that are impossible for men are possible for God." Then, thankfully, that old familiar feeling of the "peace that passes understanding" washed over me.

We found a quiet place in the waiting room, and all five of us fell on our knees and lifted up Zach in fervent prayer. Zach had a gentle spirit and was much loved by all who knew him.

It was 7:30 before we got to see him. He had so many bandages, masks, tubes, and hoses stuck in him, we couldn't recognize him. He was still in a coma, but at least he was alive and breathing. The doctors, however, didn't give us much hope that he would survive.

My thoughts rolled back to his childhood. My husband was in the military, and although we moved around a lot (including to the Philippines) I believe Zach had a happy childhood. I came from a large family, and we always enjoyed getting together at Christmas and holidays at Grandmother's house.

Sports were big in Zach's life. Tall and slim, 6'2" in high school, he naturally excelled in basketball and football. Just like I do, Zach enjoyed drawing and painting. He took a couple of art classes in high school, drew original comics and cartoons, and dreamed about pursuing a career in art.

He'd been proud of his first job, at age 14, doing volunteer work for the Red Cross. They taught him CPR and other lifesaving skills.

When he got out of school, Zach started hanging drywall. Several men in our family worked in construction — so he had learned a lot by just watching. Zach was good with his hands, and working to support himself. Like any mother, I had high hopes for my son.

Now I was sitting in a hospital waiting room, praying desperately for the Almighty God to deliver my son from evil. What on earth had happened? At times like this, I tend to start wondering, "If I had been more strict? Would things be different?"

ZACHARY: In my teen years, I regret to say, I had hung out with the wrong crowd. They introduced me to all kinds of things that I am not proud of. By age 21, friends of mine were using drugs, being killed, reported missing, and incarcerated. Hearing these things drove me away from them. That kind of living wasn't for me any longer. Yet, sorry to say, I still had a taste for alcohol.

In the year 1999, I was drinking and coming through a stop light when a dump truck ran into my car. My head went through the windshield. My face was ripped apart. The damage to the car and to my body was so severe, only the supernatural could allow me to walk away in one piece. That's when I knew I had been spared by God.

I was hospitalized for a long time. My left eye was completely closed, and doctors thought I would be blind on that side. However, within months I was healed, and one could barely notice that I had been in an accident! It was definitely by the grace of God. From that time on, I made sure that I stayed in prayer. I prayed that God would deliver me from any desire to ever touch booze again.

So I was sober and well-intentioned, the night I drove out to Bladensburg. It was no surprise to me that we arrived safely, but as I hopped out of the Jeep to use the bathroom at a store across the street, four guys — from out of nowhere — rushed and attacked me. I fought back for a few minutes, but...They pounded me till everything turned grayish white. My body felt strangely warm. I had a sensation of being suspended in air. For a long time, I felt like I was kind of floating, with my face downward. The next thing I knew (several days later) I was in the Maryland University Shock Trauma Hospital in Baltimore. Three nurses were standing over me.

They filled me in. I had been shot and robbed. I was completely paralyzed from my mid-chest down. The only body parts that I could move were my neck and arms. The bullet had struck my neck, traveled through the spinal cord, shattered the sixth and seventh vertebrae, severed an artery, and exited from my right shoulder blade. My scars tell me that I probably fell down, and they shot me while I was down.

Once they explained to me what had happened and I started remembering the events, I knew that it was only because of the grace of God and my mother's prayers that I was still alive.

WANDA: Zach had six surgeries, and his heart stopped beating four times! When Cedric Strout (a Christian minister and friend) heard this, he gave Zach the last rites. But I wasn't worried. I know the power of prayer!

Zach survived! After five months in acute surgical care, Zach was transferred to James Lawrence Kernan Hospital, an orthopedic and rehabilitation facility in Baltimore. Dr. York was his chief doctor at Kernan. Zach was eventually discharged on June 11, 2009. He is a quadriplegic. He is on fire for our God. I am praying and believing the Lord will eventually give him the use of his whole body. Zach's artistic talent lives on. Even after he'd lost full use of his limbs, he painted a beautiful paint-by-numbers picture for me; I treasure it to this day.

ZACHARY: I know I owe God an overwhelming amount of gratitude. For me to have survived what I went through, God has got to be pure love.

I tried to forgive the person who shot me, and that was not easy. Of course I was angry. But through prayer and with time, my anger diminished. Now I don't hold a grudge against anyone. God also gave me the heart to forgive the kid (Steve) for leaving me for dead, even though I never saw him again. I thank God for Mom who taught me to say the Lord's Prayer when I was just a little kid: "Forgive us our debts, as we forgive our debtors." (Matthew 6:12) And she taught me the 23rd Psalm.

I thank God for Vacation Bible School, where I learned John 3:16.

I am just plain thankful, and I'm praying that God will continue to show me the purpose He has for my life. I'm so grateful for the opportunity to give glory to God in this book. I pray my testimony will bring others to salvation, so they can avoid messing up their lives like I did.

Epilogue

Zach goes everywhere in his motor-driven wheelchair. Public transportation is a huge blessing. Zach's been to shopping centers and movie theaters. He's been to downtown Washington, D. C., to the Washington Monument and museums, and to the zoo in Baltimore. Best of all, he attends church on a regular basis. If you think you spot him on the street, just mention "Jesus" or the "Almighty One," and you will recognize Zach by his smile.

The Story of
Damon Journee

As told by Damon

I was trapped in my wheelchair for three days during the Katrina Flood. The water was up to my shoulders. It was filthy, full of germs and still rising. I was nearly dead from exposure and hunger before someone found me.

His voice was barely audible, five rows behind me during our Saturday morning Bible Study. HOW TO OVERCOME STRESS was the topic for study, and everyone was invited to participate in the discussion. When I turned around to find out who was speaking, I saw Damon Journee for the first time. His slender body sort of draped over the wheelchair like a discarded wet towel. One arm hung loosely at his side. Although his head leaned painfully to one side, his eyes were bright with new life.

One of our church members worked at the nursing home where Damon lived and had been giving Bible studies to Damon (at lunchtime). A member with a pickup truck had brought him to church that morning. Later, I had a chance to talk to him briefly, and learned that his Katrina flood experience was nothing compared to the rest of his story. I wondered why two of his front teeth were missing, but I decided to wait until I knew him better before inquiring.

Not only was it a miracle that Damon lived to tell the story, it truly is a remarkable testimony of God's amazing grace. I will let Damon tell the story in his own words.

Childhood

I was born in 1973 in New Orleans. When I was only one year old, my father got shot in the spine. Mother told me later that he was fooling around with another woman who found out he was married, flew into a rage, and shot him in the back. Although Dad was now confined to a wheelchair, he still ran a thriving business — selling crack cocaine and marijuana, and arranging the affairs of local prostitutes. He also had a legitimate business training horses and dogs for the big-time gamblers in New Orleans. He was highly respected for his ability to make so much money, and the most popular "ladies of the night" adored him.

I was really proud of my father's ability to provide for our needs. We had a good life — never felt neglected. We always had good clothes, good food, and plenty of toys at Christmas. My family was the envy of the neighborhood. Dad was cool — a no-nonsense man. In other words, Dad was king of his domain. He laid down the law in our house, and he didn't care much about what others thought — not even God.

My mother was totally opposite. She was wholesome, a goin'-to-church type of woman. Of course she didn't approve of the way Dad was living, but she loved him, and I guess because he made such good money, she put up with him. Her religion caused many hot arguments in our family. She wanted to take us kids to church, but Dad said, "If they don't want to go, we shouldn't force them."

During the few times we did attend church, it made no sense to me. It's a good thing my mother knew how to pray! Otherwise, I doubt if I would be alive today. Dad often said, "The way you are living, boy, you're gonna be six feet under by the time you're 25 years old."

I saw the big money my dad made by dealing drugs, so I worked for him long enough to learn the trade. I started dealing drugs, smoking pot and drinking when I was about 13 years old. By the time I was 15, I knew enough to strike out on my own. I could afford to buy my own house, purchase a new 1987 Cadillac, and hire several apprentices and professional ladies. But I didn't have enough smarts to fool the police!

Incarceration

They got me for distribution of crack cocaine, and I was sentenced to three and a half years as a juvenile in Louisiana Training Institute.

Forty-two months in one of Louisiana's finest penal institutions just made me resolve to become one of the most successful businessmen in New Orleans. When I graduated from LTI, I was determined to work hard and earn more money than ever before. So I soon became a distributer, instead of the average street dealer.

My reputation as a smooth operator grew quickly. At only 22 years of age, I was already making up to nine grand per day! By June,'94, I had a relationship with a nice young lady and we had our first child. In August, '95, we had our second child. Things were good. I was making money hand over fist. I had no worries. I was proud of what I did. I didn't try to beat anybody. I didn't steal from anybody. I gave people what they wanted, and I respected everybody. I also demanded my respect back. I had the reputation of being a "no-tolerance" person. You know, on the street they would say, "You better not mess with Damon, or you will get your comeuppance."

I took on two partners, hired more hustlers on the street, promoted the most popular bedroom girls, and hired a couple hoods for protection. When you're in that kind of business, it's pretty much mandatory to carry a gun. There are always people hanging around who don't want to work for a living. They just want to take what you have. The competition was fierce in those days, particularly during Mardi Gras. It was good to be known that you had a gun.

A few young guys wanted to get in the game, so I helped them and got a percentage of what they sold. In '96, I got an idea from a movie called "New Jack City," and I bought a small hotel — just a rental unit. I rented five units, made the main room like the manager's apartment where I stayed. If a customer bought a package of $100, he got a free room and he could take his pick of a prostitute for that night. I always had about six girls hanging around, available. Guys worked all week and came in on pay day.

I kept a man in the hallway with a gun, and I kept another guy (with a gun) answering the door. I strung up $100 worth of jingle bells along the fence so if people tried to climb the fence, the bells would ring. People would come, spend their money, and hang with prostitutes who would smoke drugs with them. I would also pay the prostitute a few dollars. I had a good reputation in the neighborhood, and money kept rolling in. My customers felt safe. I hired partners, including my older brother.

I didn't feel right going to church while living the way I did. I felt like a hypocrite, but I wanted my daughters to have the best, so I put them in a Catholic school. Sometimes I went to church with them. I wanted to build their foundation on church. No matter how glamorous my life looked, I knew it wasn't the right way to live.

Under Fire

All the people who worked for me loved to party, and began using too much of the merchandise. Anyone under the influence of crack cocaine, booze, marijuana, or any other recreational drug, cannot properly do their job. One night, when the party broke up about 5:00 a.m., someone followed me home. Five minutes later I heard a big bang. Someone was shooting at me. I shot back a couple of times. I figured the police would hear the shots and come. One of the guys grabbed my one year-old daughter and threatened her harm. Bullets started flying. I was standing in the exact place where seventeen bullets were heading!

That's right. Seventeen bullets tore through my body. One knocked out two front teeth before exiting through the back of my neck. Another hit just below my cheek and came out behind my ear. Two bullets in the left arm, one in the right arm, and five in the torso. Two in the back severed my spinal cord. The only internal organs that were hit were my stomach and my liver. My girl saw me in the kitchen just laying in a pool of blood. She called an ambulance. I was in a coma in the hospital for four months. When I came to, the only thing I could move was my neck. After that I was in the hospital for four more months, then in rehab for eight months.

I was only 22 years old. I prayed and asked God to let me live until I was 50. It gave me strength knowing my father had started in a wheel-chair. Doctors had told him he would never walk again, but he didn't give up. He walked with a cane before he died. So I worked and worked and worked. Worked when they didn't want me to work. I figured I could defeat the odds and learn to walk again, just like my father did.

Ninety percent of my body is still numb, to this day. I am unable to feel anything from my armpits down. To get by, I have to rely on sensations inside, and my imagination. It took a lot away from me. I could no longer go to the bathroom on my own. It took away my ability to go for a walk. It took away my ability to enjoy the touch of a woman.

So now you know why I am in a wheelchair.

Trapped by Katrina, Nine Years Later

When you live in New Orleans, you get so many hurricane warnings, you hardly pay any attention. So in 2005, Katrina caught most of us by surprise. We didn't have time to vacate, so we went to my nephew's house about nine blocks from the Mississippi River. He had an upstairs apartment in a brick house, so we figured we would be safe there. When the hurricane hit, that night, the electrical power went out. We had candles, canned food, radio, and batteries, but the worst thing happened. The dams burst, and the water from the Mississippi and water from Lake Pontchartrain emptied into the city. Within one or two hours, the water rose twenty feet. We moved up to the third floor, and kicked the door in. The water was soon up to my shoulders — as I was trapped in my wheelchair. My nephew and his wife were in their twenties, but my mother — in her sixties and diabetic — was also in a wheelchair. Helicopters started coming for people who were stranded on rooftops. After three endless days, a guy with a boat picked us up from the third floor, and took us to higher ground next to the convention center. We still had to deal with two or three feet of water, and it was pitch black inside. People got raped, assaulted and robbed, and there was a shortage of food and water. It wasn't safe to stay in the convention center.

We went outside. Though the water was up to my waist, I pushed my mother's chair while sitting in my own chair. People were looting and trading jewelry and stuff for food. I was able to trade some stuff for enough food to keep Mom alive. On the third day, we saw a cousin. He stayed with us until the National Guard came on the third day. From a helicopter, they dropped five cases of water and five cases of rationed meals into a crowd of thousands of people. People were fighting for it. But me (being in a wheelchair) didn't have a chance to get any of the food or water. It's a miracle we survived.

The Lone Star

I'm not suffering from the gunshot wounds now. I suffer from the effects of sitting in that water — full of germs and bacteria — for three days. My body was so brittle you could just pull the skin off. Someone finally rescued Mom and me, and we were evacuated to Texas. I was in the hospital three or five months, then a nursing home for about seven months. When I was released, I went to live with my mother who had bought a house in Texas.

Mom had raised seven children. I was the youngest of three boys and four girls. Mom kept telling me the only way to be saved was through the Lord, but I didn't understand. I stayed with her till Mom became too sick to take care of me. She had bad diabetes and her kidneys were failing.

A New Beginning

My brother in Baltimore invited Mom to live with him. Since I was the youngest in the family, she wanted me to come to Baltimore, too. My brother knew my reputation, and he told me I could come live with him and Mom as long as I didn't sell any more drugs. I'm so glad I got to spend more time with Mom. They finally put her in a nursing home, and she passed away in November, 2009. Just before my mother died, I promised her I would make her proud of me. I have friends who prayed about it, and I decided to stop using or selling drugs or marijuana (but I didn't give up alcohol). Being drug-free is a new beginning, and that's exactly what I needed.

Fast Forward to January 2011

Here I am, Damon Journee, 38 years old, living in a cheap nursing home in Maryland. I'm stuck in my wheelchair with nothing much to do but read and think. It's a miracle that I am still living and my mind still works. I'm still paralyzed from my armpits down, but I have a little use of my arms and hands. Because of nerve damage, I can't use my fingers in my right arm, but I can feed myself, operate my wheelchair, hold a book, and talk to friends on my cell phone.

No matter how depressed I get, or how tough things seem, I still count my blessings because somewhere, someone is struggling more than me. I know, now, that most of my suffering is a consequence of the sinful life I was living. But I should have died long ago, so I thank God for giving me a second chance!

I have lots of time to think, these days, and I have been trying to figure out why God has kept me alive. For one thing, I'm pretty sure Mom's prayers had a lot to do with it.

I'm thankful for a man named Francisco. He worked in this nursing home for awhile and he became a good friend. When he had a day off from work, he would visit me and give me a Bible study. Francisco made me appreciate the Bible! It really is a wonderful book. Although I read it a lot when I was in prison, without a teacher, I couldn't understand it. I read it because it was the only book they let me have. But I was just reading words to pass the time. My mind was always focused on something else — like how I was going to make a million bucks when I got out! Well, I made plenty of money. But where did that get me? Most of it has gone to doctors, hospitals, lawyers, and the pills I have to take if I don't want the pain to keep me awake all night.

I was always a praying person. Even before I became a Christian, I used to think anyone could pray to God about anything, and He would answer. When I got into a tough situation, I would pray about it, and I think the Lord got me through it. When I was dealing drugs and I came to a place where there was a conflict, like if someone did me wrong, I would ask God what I should do. "Should I kill them, or let them go? Or should I just forget about it?" When my children were born, I prayed I would have a healthy child. Any important decision I had to make, I prayed about it. I prayed even when I was doing drugs. Even when doing shoot-outs with people, I prayed. One day I prayed, "Let me live to see 50, and every day after that I will consider extra." I always believed in God. I always respected Him.

But Francisco made me realize I used to have some really dumb ideas about prayer. He showed me in the Bible where God said, "If I regard iniquity (sin) in my heart, the Lord will not hear me." (Psalm 66:18)

One time when I was in jail and in the gym lifting weights, a preacher came and started a church meeting. I had a choice to return to my cell or stay for the church meeting. I wasn't really interested in what they were saying at the time, but we had to keep quiet while they were talking, so I started listening to what they were saying. I listened and I felt unbelievable happiness. Something like an out-of-body experience came over me. It got me to thinking, "Is this where I want to be the rest of my life? Is this what I want?" No answers, just a lot of questions for me to figure out, and that's what started me. As I thought about it, that night as I lay in bed, I felt a peace come over me, and I thought maybe it was the Holy Spirit talking to me.

A couple times when someone took me for a ride and we rode by a church on Sunday morning, I'd see people coming out of church, and they all had big smiles on their faces — kinda like people who are high on drugs. I wondered what was going on. The church that Mom took me to when I was a kid was boring. Most of the speaking was Latin. Made no sense to me! I asked Francisco why those people coming from church were laughing and smiling? He said, "When you give your life to Jesus, you become part of God's family...and then when you go to a church where everybody loves God, it's like a big happy family reunion." He also showed me a verse in the Bible that says: "The joy of the Lord is your strength." (Nehemiah 8:10)

I asked Francisco why God keeps me alive. He told me that God is keeping me alive to be a witness for Him, to be a testimony of His amazing grace. He taught me the meaning of GRACE in a way that's easy to remember:

G = **G**od's
R = **R**eward
A = **A**t
C = **C**hrist's
E = **E**xpense

He said God's grace is all about His love for us. He taught me a verse that most Christians know: "God so loved the world that He gave His only begotten Son that whosoever believes in Him shall not perish, but will have everlasting life." (John 3:16)

I was really confused about that. I told Francisco, "All my life I've heard that only good people can go to heaven. I've done some terrible things in my life, so how can I go to heaven? But that verse says all you have to do is believe in Jesus and anyone can go to heaven. Makes no sense to me." He explained it this way:

God put Adam and Eve in a beautiful garden and told them if they ate from the Tree of Life they could live forever. But, He said, "Don't eat from the tree of Knowledge of Good and Evil or you will die!" Satan lied to Eve and tempted her to eat of the wrong tree. Ever since then, everybody who descended from Adam and Eve inherited their sinful nature. The Bible says, "All have sinned (Jesus was the exception) and come short of the glory of God. The wages of sin is death, but the gift of God is eternal life." Jesus' Father was the Holy Spirit and Jesus' mother was Mary, who was a virgin until Jesus was born. That's why Jesus did not inherit a sinful nature. Therefore, He was qualified to give up His life to save us — by taking the punishment we deserve — when he died on the cross at Calvary. But, as I guess you know, on the third day, Jesus came out of His grave! That's why we celebrate Easter. That's a miracle that probably no one can really understand. We just have to believe it by faith. And the neat thing is — even if you don't have the faith to believe it — you can ask God to give you faith. Faith is a gift from God! And the Bible says when we confess our sins to God, He will forgive us and wash away all our sins. That's how God is preparing us to live forever with Him in heaven.

Bible experts say all the terrible things that are happening these days — like earthquakes, floods, famines, pestilence — are warning signs that the end of the world and Judgment Day is coming soon. Evil-doers will be punished, and the Lord Jesus is coming back to take everyone who loves Him to heaven.

Hallelujah! We will get a brand new, pain-free body. Wow! I will be able to run, jump, and dance again. No need for wheelchairs or hospitals in heaven. I'm hoping to see my mother, but I kinda doubt if my Dad will be there. But the best part is...we will see Jesus!

The Meaning and Purpose of Life

Anybody who reads this story, I can tell you one thing for sure — If God can save a loser like me, He can save anybody!

I'm hoping and praying that people will read this story about my wasted life and learn from my mistakes. Sure, I made big bucks, but look what it did for me. I was a big shot — living high on the hog for a few years — but now I can't do anything by myself. I must depend on others to take care of me. There's very little I can do for anyone else except to warn them: Don't ignore God any longer. It's dangerous!

Ask God to shine the light of His word into your heart to reveal your sins. Then ask God to forgive your sins and give you the power of the Holy Spirit to kick Satan out of your life for good, and give you the desire to live a life that is pleasing to God. Find a church where people love the Lord and, most of all, where the Bible is taught as the Living Word of God!

If it's possible, make restitution for people who you have harmed. Pray about that. I read in the Bible about a crooked little tax collector named Zacchaeus. When he fell in love with Jesus, he said he was going to pay back (four times over) to people he had stolen from. Now that's restitution!

I've had a tough life, but I believe the Lord put me here for a purpose, and maybe I had to go through these things to fulfill His purpose. So if I had it to do over again, I don't think I would change anything. I believe you gotta play the hand you were dealt.

I pray that many young people will read my story and learn from my mistakes. You can fool a lot of people, but don't even try to mess with God. Just remember — He loves you more than you can ever understand, and He is not willing for you to perish. Walk with Him — and He will walk with you.

The Story of
Tina Black

As told by Tina

"Every time I imagine someone with severe pain, I think of my sister-in-law, Tina. Tina would stand up in the back of the church, then sit down, then stand up again."

— *My brother-in-law David, referencing me in his sermon*

I have been going to church since I was in preschool. I was really blessed to have a mother who always took us, no matter what. When I was about eight years old, we were living in Clinton, Maryland, and I saw a movie called *A Thief in the Night*. It scared me stiff! So that evening, I sat by my window and talked to God. I asked the Lord to forgive me of my sins and come into my heart! That's how I received Jesus Christ as my Lord and Savior. I fell in love with Him. I started reading my Bible and praying. Over the years, I have read the Bible through, year after year. I try to pray all the time, no matter where I am or what I am doing. The Lord has always been there to hear and help me.

My suffering began in 1996. The accident took place on Marshall Hall Road in Bryans Road, Maryland. That's between Fort Washington and Indian Head, Maryland. My husband Tim and our son Colton and I were going house hunting that day. We were driving our 1974 Plymouth Duster, and the other fellow was driving his F-150 pickup truck. Tim had actually spoken to him, earlier, at the end of a cul-de-sac. The man had been sitting in the back of his truck, drinking beer with a few of his friends. Tim had asked if anyone knew the location of a house for sale. (I had pointed them out to my husband because the man looked like my uncle.) Later on, while we were looking at the house, this same man drove to the store to get more beer.

We had just finished a walk-through and were leaving the house. The man was coming back down the road. His vehicle crossed the yellow line and hit us, head on. His truck slammed into our car and knocked us to the side of the road. The engine and transmission were driven back into the firewall, and buckled the floor. Since I wasn't wearing a seat belt, the momentum threw me forward; spun me over in my seat; and struck me on the left side of my face as I slammed into the side of my door. When I tried to get up, I tasted blood. It felt like I had a mouth full of broken teeth. I discovered it was glass, when I spit into my hand. I pushed myself off the seat and looked back at my twenty-two month-old son. He was still in his car seat. The backseat itself, along with the car seat, had unhooked from the floor and slammed forward into our front seat. It was by the grace of God that his little legs and feet were not crushed or hurt in any way. He was perfectly fine. I then tried to turn over onto my back and sit up in my seat. My husband looked like he was dead. Part of the windshield frame on the left side of the car had broken loose and smacked him on his forehead. His head was bleeding profusely. I kept yelling, "Tim, wake up! Tim, wake up!" As I was screaming, I saw smoke coming from the front of our car on Tim's side. I was still in shock and didn't realize that my left femur was shattered, internally. The bottom part (still in the skin) was pushed over and upward toward the outside of my leg. I thank God that none of this was registering in my brain at all.

Witnesses later said that the drunk driver threw the beer cans out of his truck (getting rid of some of the evidence). Then he got out of his truck, which was still hooked to our car, and came over to the driver side of our car, where my husband was seated.

The drunk man, starting to see the smoke, pulled at my husband's side of the car. He could not get the door open. I found out (two years later) that this man had had several alcohol-related accidents, before. As soon as the neighbors heard the loud car crash, many of them immediately thought, "I bet it's him." Sure enough, it was him.

Bystanders told him, "Don't move her," but the man ignored them and motioned to me to unlock the door. When I unlocked the door,

I was still in shock and still screaming for my husband. The drunken man told me (in a normal tone of voice) "Shut up." He then removed me from the car, and placed me by the roadside. My left femur bone — halfway down — was now twisted toward the middle of my body, with my foot sticking straight up in the air, while I was lying flat on the road. When he moved me out of our car, this just made matters worse for my leg.

I asked a lady, "Can you please check on my son and husband? I think my husband is dead." Meanwhile, the drunk driver was getting Colton out of our car. He left him in the car seat, and put Colton next to me. I told the lady, "Ma'am, something is wrong with my leg. I can't put my leg down." She said, "It's okay, Honey." Nothing was registering because I was still in shock, and Tim was still in the car.

The paramedics quickly arrived. When they started up the "jaws of life," Tim moved. Praise the Lord! He had been unconscious, this whole time. He had no trouble sliding over onto the passenger side, where he got out of the car. Tim said, "I'm okay, Tina. Your leg is broken, but you'll be fine." I said, "Okay, honey. I love you."

The paramedics were alarmed when they saw my leg still sticking straight up in the air (while I was lying flat on my back). One of them held my head very still and said, "You scream as loud as you want to." The other paramedic then moved my leg (that was twisted inward) to an outward position, straightening it. Then they set it back on the ground. The shock of it all disappeared quickly. As the pain set in, I started to grasp the fact that my leg was broken. Meanwhile, the paramedics didn't know that the bone had shattered and splintered-off inside my leg. This was a serious problem. I was told later that, while they were repositioning my leg, the splintered-off piece could have severed my femoral artery. If that had happened, I could have died within fifteen minutes. Oh, what God protects us from that we don't even know about!

Tim and Colton were taken by ambulance to Fort Washington Hospital, but they took me by helicopter to Prince George's Trauma Center. When I arrived, they put me in traction. To do this procedure, they had to numb the area and drill a hole through my leg. They inserted a pin through the lower part of my left leg — just below my knee. I kept telling them, "It's not numb!" They replied, "We still have to go through." I kept screaming the whole time, "Jesus, please help me!" I was having severe muscle spasms by this time, and they weren't letting up.

The next day, when they learned that my insurance would not pay for the surgery at Prince George's Hospital, they arranged to transfer me by ambulance to Holy Cross Hospital in Silver Spring, Maryland. This is where they performed my femur surgery. While getting ready for transport (with my leg still in traction) the nursing assistant at Prince George's Hospital was trying to fit my bed into the elevator to go down to the ambulance. He tried three times to get me into the elevator. I cried out, "Please measure the bed and the space in the elevator." The bed was too long for the elevator, and the traction weights were swinging — causing my leg to have severe muscle spasms, one after the other. I was still screaming, "Jesus, please help me!" I'm told that my screaming sent a security officer to the elevator. He thought a woman was being attacked! Finally, a nurse shortened the bed, and they were able to squeeze the bed into the elevator.

At Holy Cross the next day, I was rolled to the operating room. I remember saying to Tim, "I love you," then I was fast asleep from the anesthetic. When I woke up in ICU, I told the nurse I couldn't go through with the surgery. She said, "Tina, the surgery has already been done." I said, "Okay," and dropped off to sleep again. The doctor tried morphine and Demerol for the pain. However, I had an allergic reaction to both of these medicines. Morphine made me have severe itching with a rash all over. The Demerol made me vomit, over and over again.

After three days in the hospital, they moved me to a rehabilitation/nursing center in Wheaton, Maryland, where I spent another sixteen days, or so. Here, they tried to teach me to walk again, but it wouldn't sink into my brain. So I kept saying, "Lord Jesus, please help me to use my brain signals to get my leg to move forward." I was now in a wheelchair with nothing to do, so I went through all the hallways, and witnessed to everyone I saw — doctors and nurses included. I told them all about my wonderful Savior.

I was finally discharged home. We stayed at my father and mother-in-law's home, where a nurse visited regularly to help me exercise the left leg. It sure was a blessing to have my in-laws there to take good care of us for about a month and a half. They were a big help to Tim and me when Tim had to return to work and I needed someone to help me with Colton.

Two months later, I began to feel sorry for myself. "Why do I have to go through this, Lord? Why does one leg have to be shorter than the other, and now I have to wear a shoe lift?" What had happened during surgery at Holy Cross Hospital is that the surgeon had taken me out of traction and removed the pin (which they had inserted at Prince George's Trauma Center). The surgeons should have (according to another orthopedic doctor's opinion) inserted a new pin at the base of the steel rod (inside the femur bone) above the knee. This would have secured the bottom part of my leg and kept it in place. A pin wasn't inserted there to stop the lower part of my leg from moving upward. The rod in my leg kept feeling like it was jamming into my knee. When I started to bear weight on my left side, the leg would get shorter and shorter — causing a one-inch difference in the length of my legs. The surgeon told me it was just my imagination. He also stated that maybe I was just born like that. When the second orthopedic doctor measured my legs, he found an inch difference. He also assured me that I was not born that way, and it was not my imagination that the leg was moving upward whenever I would bear weight on it.

I learned that Maryland law allows five years to file a medical malpractice claim for mishaps like this. After getting the other orthopedic doctor's opinion about the pin that should have been inserted, it was two months too late. Now, every time I buy a pair of shoes, I need an inch shoe-lift added to my left shoe.

My self-pity didn't last too long because one day — when I went to pick up my special shoe — I saw something significant: The lady in the car parked next to me got out of her vehicle. As I watched, I realized she was there to pick up her plastic legs. I immediately gasped, "Father God, forgive me for complaining. I need to be grateful that I still have my leg and that I can walk now." I can do all things through Christ which strengthens me (Philippians 4:13). This scripture really helped me get through it all.

By 1997, I was pregnant with our second baby, Leah. While I was pregnant, the doctors discovered that my pelvic area had been shifted to the right during the impact of the car accident. The baby was riding extremely low, and as a result, I was put in a wheelchair and on bedrest for the last five months of my pregnancy.

Months rolled into years. It was now 1998. One night, on the way home from La Plata Baptist Church, where I had taken Colton to an AWANA program (similar to scouts, but Bible-based) I stopped at a red light at the intersection of Port Tobacco Road and Maryland Route 301. Traffic was crisscrossing in front of me, and when I looked up in my rearview mirror — WHAM — another accident! The policeman said the driver was drunk! He had just come from a bar, and he was probably unconscious when he hit me. He was going about fifty-five miles per hour on impact. Like most drunk drivers, he was able to get out of his car. I had my seatbelt on. Colton (four and a half years old) and Leah (ten months old) were both in their car-seats.

I tried to get out of our Aerostar van, but I could not get my driver's door open. My children were screaming! I crawled to the passenger side to exit, and when I opened the children's sliding door, it fell! Thank God, the kids seemed to be alright — just terribly frightened. I was panicked and in shock once again. I wasn't even concerned about myself because my mind was on them. They took us all by ambulance to Physicians Memorial Hospital in La Plata, Maryland.

I asked the policeman if the driver was being charged for drunk driving. He said, "Yes, Ma'am. He had a 2.8 alcohol level." I found out he was on parole when he hit us, and had blown a 3.5 in a previous accident. I wanted to make sure he was charged, since the 1996 driver had been charged for the accident, but not for being drunk. (His father was a police officer, apparently, and got him off the DUI charge.)

At the hospital, they discovered my tailbone had been jammed forward at a 90° angle. My lower back was messed up again, and I had whiplash. (I have to sit on cushions, wherever I go.)

In 1999, I had my third baby, Aaron. I was in a wheelchair and on bed rest, again. By this time, I was told by my doctor to never go to a chiropractor; that my body was too far gone; that it would only make matters worse. This doctor also said, "Be prepared...someday you may be crippled from all the trauma to your body." I was also told by my doctors that because of this (and my high blood pressure) trying to bear more children could kill me and the baby. This really upset me. We wanted more children! I regret to say that in those days, we didn't have the kind of faith that we do now. If we had had enough faith in the Lord (no matter what) He could and would have taken care of everything.

The doctor gave me pain pills, muscle relaxers, anti-inflammatory pills, and blood pressure meds. Then, they sent me to a pain management specialist. The verdict: "We're sorry, Ma'am, but there is nothing else we can do for you." Oh, but I knew Someone who could!

I then called my brother-in-law, who was the pastor of the King James Baptist Church in Nanjemoy, Maryland. He was leading a tent revival at the time. I said, "David, I am in so much pain; I feel like I can only move my eyeballs. Could the men in the church pray over me, anoint me with oil, and ask God to heal me?" That night, the men prayed, and I was anointed with oil. The next morning, a lot of the pain was gone! I knew God had touched me.

Through the following years, I still dealt with pain, but not the locked-up muscle pain like I had battled that night when they prayed for me. Before that night, I could not pick up my children or stand up to do dishes, and I had been homeschooling my children from my bed.

In November of 2006, we moved to West Virginia. One day in December of 2009, I was teaching my youngest son, Aaron, when I felt something pull in my back! I said to myself, "Mmm...that felt pretty good." But when I stood up, I cried out, "Oh Lord, please help me!" The pain in my back was terrible. After I told my children what to do for school, I walked slowly to my bedroom...where I stayed for weeks. I couldn't sit on the commode or pick up a jar of peanut butter, and I was once again schooling the children from my bed. I had to lie flat most of the time. All this lasted until April 2010.

I talked with God while literally getting down on my face, and I said, "Oh Lord, if it's Your will for me to be crippled for the rest of my life, I'm willing to accept it. However, if it's Your will, dear Lord, please have mercy on me and heal me. Father, when I go to church, I don't want people, Lord, to see the pain on my countenance. I want them to see Your joy, but I want to show Your glory, as well. I want to be a help to my family and to others. You are the final authority and the great physician, and I know You can heal me."

One night, after I'd been lying in bed for nine weeks, Tim was massaging my back. When I moved to stretch, we both heard a loud POP. Tim blurted out, "What was that?" I said, "That was my lower back!" So, I asked him to massage it again. "Oh my goodness, the Lord has healed me after fourteen years!" It felt like He'd popped that sacrum bone (the triangular-shaped bone just above the tailbone) back into its place. With all the x-rays I have had (I'm glowing, by now) and the doctor appointments, I was never told that my sacrum was "out." All those years, I had felt as if I was walking around like a stringed puppet in that area. Now I knew why! I kept thanking God for healing me. I can't thank Him enough!

In Romans 5:3-5, the Bible says, "And not only so, but we glory in tribulations also: knowing that tribulation worketh patience; and patience experience; and experience, hope." What if I hadn't had hope in Jesus Christ? I would still be in tremendous pain, and I'd have nothing.

April 2011 — I can walk, climb stairs, ride a bicycle, walk in the woods with our children, wash the dishes and prepare food. All of the things I once took for granted, now seem so precious. I remember reading about the Apostle Paul and the thorn in his flesh. He asked God three times to remove it. But God answered: "My grace is sufficient for thee: for my strength is made perfect in weakness" (II Corinthians 12:9a). This taught me that it's not "all about me!" It's about how He can use me. If I'd never had a problem, would I have learned about faith?

My sweet husband, Tim, has been such a blessing. He has helped me not just physically, but spiritually, mentally, and emotionally. I also thank God for my precious children. They have helped me with meals, cleansing, and keeping up their schoolwork through it all.

I had felt sorry for them because all they'd known was Mama in pain. I was asked at church, one day, "Tina, why do you think God took fourteen years to heal you?" I replied, "Maybe it was for my children — so that they would see the faith of Jesus, and the glory of God." My granddaddy-in-law once said, "If you have Jesus Christ, you have everything!" I don't want pity from anyone. I just want others to see Jesus in me because He did it all! Romans 8:28 sums it up: And we know that all things work together for good to them that love God, to them who are the called, according to his purpose.

Epilogue

The drunk driver in the 1998 accident was supposed to get four years of jail time. But he only received eight months. I found out that he lived just two streets over from us. It took me ten years to get over my anger from those two accidents. I knew I had to forgive and forget. I knew that God had put me in this position to be a witness for Him. So in time, He impressed upon me to sign the back of two gospel tracts, "Someone who cares about your soul." Then I sent them to both of the drunk drivers. God showed me that it's more important for their souls to be saved from their sins and hell, than for me to be vindicated during this short time on earth. This earth is only temporary.

The Story of
Dave Harman

As told by Dave and his wife Helen

DAVE: I was born in Fremont, Northern Ohio, in 1955; raised and educated as a Roman Catholic. I enlisted in the US Army, took basic training at Fort Dix, and moved to Fort Devins, Massachusetts, for advanced Army Intelligence Training.

I was a typical 18 year-old punk soldier — drinking; chasing skirts; the whole nine yards. Christians began witnessing to me, and I eventually listened. Someone invited me to go to a Billy Graham movie. I went forward at the altar call, and was saved on April 9, 1975. From that day on, I was a follower of the Lord Jesus!

Helen and I met at a Christian retreat center where I was a youth counselor on weekends. The Lord told me that she was the girl He chose for me, so two weeks later I proposed.

I got out of the army on June 20, 1978, and we were married in August. We lived temporarily in Manassas, Virginia. Then we moved to Tennessee for a year to help a friend plant a church.

IBM hired me in 1982, and we adopted our daughter, Beth, in 1985. The job moved me around quite a bit — First, Manassas, then Detroit, where I was a Customer Support Representative. While there, we had a great church family in a large Assembly of God Church with about 5000 members. I was promoted to be a business analyst in Washington, D.C., so we moved back to Manassas. In 1992 we moved to Raleigh, North Carolina.

Around 1996, I started getting some weird symptoms — frequent dizzy spells. I started going to my family doctor when numbness set in from my ankles down — couldn't feel a thing!

We discovered it was Multiple Sclerosis. No one has a clue what causes Multiple Sclerosis (MS). Scientists don't know if it's viral, bacterial, or environmental. The earliest case on record is from 1822. They diagnose MS by process of elimination. There is a long list of diseases that it could be, and they test you for each one of these. They can do a spinal tap and look for evidence of dissolved myelin. Myelin is the insulation that covers your nerves, and what happens in MS is that your body attacks itself — it's an autoimmune disease — and spots of myelin are removed from the nerve. It's like an electric wire — when you remove the insulation, it causes a short circuit.

Sometimes I would be feeling fine, walking through the mall when all of a sudden, my legs would stop working. Then I would have to just wait one, two, or three hours until I could move my legs enough to just hobble. Invariably, the rest of the day or week was pretty much shot. I felt kind of like the Energizer Bunny with a dollar-store battery.

I started going to the doctor in December 1997. He set me up with a neurologist. The first doctor visit was disappointing. We felt that our questions weren't being answered, and that we were an imposition. We were really scared. The MRI showed multiple lesions on my brain. During the process of diagnosing, I went numb from the waist down. I had a terrible time trying to walk, so we bought a cane. One of the symptoms is extreme fatigue — I was too tired to move and too tired to think!

We transferred to Dr. Kevin Kahn at the University of North Carolina Neurosciences Hospital. He was a wonderful man who did his best to help treat the disease.

HELEN: Over seven years, I slowly lost my husband, and Elizabeth lost her father. The man who the army had sent to Military Intelligence School because of his high IQ was now not able to finish sentences. The man who was a business analyst for 19 years with IBM was no longer able to sign a restaurant check. He would get up in the morning with no idea of what he needed to do on that day. I would write a list for him, and then would have to phone him several times during the day to remind him to look at the list. On bad days, I had to remind him to eat lunch. Then he would ask what there was in the house to eat.

He couldn't open the fridge, see luncheon meat and think to make himself a sandwich.

DAVE: I was a business analyst. I wrote programs to analyze sales, quotas, and objectives, but now I'd reached a point where I couldn't do any of that. So IBM sent me home on disability. By that time, I was in an electric wheelchair. Whenever we went somewhere, I had to have it. The first time my legs stopped working, they put one of those heparin locks in my arm so they could just hook up an IV without repeated venipuncture. For a week I was making trips to the clinic to receive Solu-Medrol, which is a heavy-duty steroid. I received only a dose or two because the side-effects of this medication can be severe.

So I lost my job. I did not leave willingly. They forced me out. I can understand that. I wasn't doing the job. Disability pay was about half of what I was earning. A couple weeks after being let go, I had a nervous breakdown and spent a week in the University of North Carolina Neurosciences Hospital; the psychiatric ward. Doctor Kahn was the admitting doctor. They started me on drugs that made me better able to handle the depression, and I ended up under the care of my family doctor (Thomas Weber) and a psychiatrist (Randall Grigg). Dr. Grigg was managing my medications. I took all three of the ABC drugs: Avonex, Betaseron, and Copaxone. These drugs were injectable, and they slowed the progression of the disease. Since there is no cure for MS, the prognosis was grim. There would always be relapses, and my relapses were strange.

At one point my eyes were really messed-up. I was just seeing black spots. I was going a neural ophthalmologist at UNC regularly. He was a teaching doctor, so one day he said, "You won't mind if I bring some students to see you, will you?" He brought in five or six interns and said to them, "You guys may never again see anything like this. You'd better take a look." I thought, "Well! I'm so glad I could be of some assistance!"

During a relapse, sometimes I would lose the use of my arms or legs. At other times, it was just uncontrollable shaking that came over me.

More weird things happened to my eyes. Sometimes I'd just see dots. Other times, I'd see something like flocks of birds. Sometimes, at night with low light, I would perceive my surroundings as similar to stop-motion photography.

If we got a bill at a restaurant for ten dollars, I could not calculate a ten-percent tip! People would approach and talk to me, and I couldn't understand them.

HELEN: Now all the decisions became my responsibility, like how to save money. What company do we choose for health insurance? How do we help Beth with her learning difficulties? Can the dryer be fixed or shall we buy a new one? I could not talk to Dave about the stress I was under with all these responsibilities because he would become too upset.

Our family members tried to help by painting the inside of our home and building a new front porch. Dave appreciated the support, but overall he felt less of a man because he could not take care of his own family. Dave said he worried that he would not be able to protect his family should the need arise.

Most heartbreaking to me was when I realized he could not remember portions of our life together. One of my secret fears was that he would not remember how I looked on our wedding day.

When Dave reached a point where he could no longer work, he had a nervous breakdown. It was unbelievably hard for Beth and me to watch Dave get locked in every night and wave goodbye through the window of the hospital ward. How do you explain this to a thirteen-year-old?

Dave took two antidepressants a day, and remained in treatment twice a month for five years. The medication only took the edge off his severe depression. Dave said it was like living in a black pit! In October 2003, Dave woke me up, one morning, saying he did not want to be alone. Then he lay down beside me and started sobbing. All I could do was hold his head and pray. He cried for an hour. He had lost all hope for the future and was just waiting to die!

On his darkest days, he could not form a prayer in his head. On good days, he could only pray the Lord's Prayer because that was part of him. If we attended a one-hour church service, I could see his complexion turning gray (about half way through the service). This would generally wipe out the rest of Sunday. He had no energy to be interested in anything; not even a conversation.

Every day, he was impacted by many different physical symptoms — dizzy spells where he would have to grab something to keep from falling. These dizzy spells would wake him up from a sound sleep. His hands shook. If he did a repetitive motion, such as cutting up food or using a screwdriver, his hands would stop working. In the evening, his legs would spasm and jerk. You could see his legs lift up more than a foot above the seat of his recliner. Walking across our gently-sloping yard felt like climbing a mountain. When we went through crowded malls and stores in his electric wheelchair, he felt humiliated and snubbed by sales clerks.

Dave also suffered from vision problems every day. Occasionally he saw things that were not there. Sometimes he had "trailing images." If he moved his hand, then he would see ten hands following behind. This subsided after a couple hours.

Two of his main problems were fatigue and heat. If his temperature became slightly high, his symptoms would worsen. At times, he became so weak he could hardly hold his head up.

DAVE: I was wondering where God was. I didn't know what was going on. The meetings at church were exuberant, but it got to where I couldn't take the noise. I can remember hearing about people who went to faith healers like Benny Hinn, and I remember (in the '70s) there was a big movement called, "Name It and Claim it!" But I can remember thinking, "It's not the way Jesus healed people." Eventually, we started visiting a Lutheran church. It was more of a liturgical service, very quiet and reserved.

One day the family all got together in Virginia, at my brother-in-law's house in Remington. We were all invited to go to a place of worship called, "The Holy Way" in Bealeton, Virginia. This was not a church, just a lovely, secluded place in the country. Christians of all denominations would go just for fellowship, to seek the Lord. I was told they had big couches where I could comfortably sit. Just to be polite, I agreed to go. I was saying to myself, "I spend most of my time sitting in my chair or on a couch, anyway. So I guess I can sit anywhere."

I was able to climb the stairs, half crawling and hobbling. (The biggest problem was dizziness and balance.) There was much singing and praising. Worshipers were sharing scripture and testimonies. But I was just sitting on the couch (as usual) just waiting to die, with no interest or understanding of anything. Without warning, Herry and Mike were suddenly standing in front of me. Herry Stubbe was the director of The Holy Way. Originally from Indonesia, Herry was adopted and brought to the U.S. by a missionary named Edwin Stubbe. Mike Chapman was an Episcopal priest, and the director of The Holy Way in Moravian Falls, North Carolina.

Herry cut to the chase. "Would it be okay if we prayed for you?" he asked.

Mike added, "Do you have a fearful heart?"

I didn't understand what Mike was asking.(Helen filled me in later.)

My wife replied for me and said, "Yes, he has a fearful heart."

I don't remember exactly what they prayed since I was in a dark pit of depression. My first clue that something marvelous was happening was the sense that the lights had come on — I no longer felt depressed. I started laughing!

Mike Chapman had his hand on my head, and he asked, "Brother, do you have gel or something in your hair?"

"No," I replied.

"You feel like you're melting."

My brother-in-law, Pat, was sitting on the other side of the room. Realizing that something was happening, he headed in our direction. He later told me, "As I came across the room and got closer to you, I felt like I had entered a cloud of God's glory. I couldn't even stand! I just fell to my knees."

HELEN: When Mike and Herry walked across the room toward us, I didn't know what they were doing until Mike asked Dave if they could pray for him. These were the first words Herry and/or Mike had said to Dave. Then they began to pray, speaking words of healing. Mike stopped praying and said he had a scripture for Dave, so he went back to his chair for his Bible. He read a portion of Isaiah, 33:6 to Dave. "The fear of the Lord is his treasure." Mike then flipped the page and read Isaiah, 35:3 & 4, "Strengthen ye the weak hands, and confirm the feeble knees. Say to them that are of a fearful heart, Be strong, fear not: behold, your God will come with vengeance, even God with a recompense; he will come and save you." It was then that Mike asked Dave, "Do you have a fearful heart?"

Dave was unable to answer, and looked to me. I said, "Yes. Dave has a fearful heart."

Mike told Dave, "Turn it over to God. Lay everything at God's feet." Then Mike placed his hands on Dave's head and Dave began to pray, turning everything over to God. As Dave prayed you could see his countenance changing. All my family was able to see the difference in his face as he was praying. When Mike told Dave his head felt like it was melting, we realized that this was God's anointing.

At that moment, I knew that God had healed Dave's heart, mind, and spirit!

DAVE: That night, Helen phoned our daughter, Elizabeth. She tried to tell her what had happened, but she was crying so much, she couldn't make herself understood. "Calm down, Mom," Elizabeth urged. "Calm down."

"I'm trying to tell you something has happened to your dad. You will be able to look at him and see the difference. There's a noticeable change in his countenance. You can see the change! Remember before... how he always looked gray? Wait till you see him! You won't believe he's the same person!"

All I knew when we left The Holy Way was that I was no longer depressed! If that had been the extent of my healing, that would have been enough. Awesome!

The next morning I got up early, wanting to make a cup of coffee. Pat and Peg use filtered water that's delivered in huge, blue bottles. I'm usually not aware of anything much until I've had my first cup of coffee. Since the water bottle was empty, I stepped out on the porch and picked up a full bottle of water, and carried it into the kitchen. I remember my other brother-in-law, Bill, sitting there watching me. He had a jaw-dropping, eye-popping, incredible look on his face. He was watching a man who was previously only barely able to walk!

As soon as I'd had my coffee, we were ready to drive back home. And I drove. I drove a car for the first time in about five years. Gradually, over the next few days, I realized I had zero symptoms of MS!

The whole time I was sick, Helen couldn't go to church without shedding tears of exhaustion. She remembers just wanting to lie in God's hand; to rest in His presence. When we arrived at The Holy Way meeting, she was emotionally in a very dry place. But when Helen joined the worship, she was so struck by God's presence that she wept. When Mike and Herry came across the room, none of us realized they were coming to us until they stepped around the coffee table to approach me. Helen tells of the overwhelming feeling she had at that moment. "O my gosh! God knows how bad we're hurting, and He has sent these two men to pray for us." Helen figured they would pray for us, and we would feel a little better. No one had any idea what was about to happen. As they prayed for me, all my wife could do was weep.

DAVE: After praying for me, Mike and Herry had turned and prayed for Helen. Mike then said he had a word from God for her. "You feel like your prayers have been going up to heaven and bouncing back down, falling into the depths of the ocean. But God wants you to know He has answered your prayers because you have been faithful."

"I hadn't been aware of what I had been praying," Helen admits. "It wasn't like we had an altar set up at home, and I'd been kneeling at this altar all the time, or lighting candles, or any of the other things you hear of people doing. But when Mike prophesied, I recalled all the times when I was standing at the sink washing dishes — or driving the car — and I would just think, 'Lord, I want my husband back. Please give my husband back to me.'"

HELEN: After the service, Dave told me he was going downstairs to talk with Mike. I was aware that I was watching Dave go down the stairs, and I was not the least bit worried about him falling! I will never forget that feeling. Later, I joined Dave downstairs and watched him hold the longest conversation in seven years. Dave had been telling Mike that he had MS, and Mike was stunned. In later conversations, Mike shared, "If I had known you had MS, I never would have had the nerve to pray for you. My sister-in-law had MS, and she committed suicide."

Herry expressed similar sentiments. His stepmother had died from MS years before.

DAVE: As we were driving home, that day, Helen said to me, "I can't wrap my mind around this much love." She knew there was absolutely nothing we had done to deserve this. She knew it was just God's love. Talking about it during that drive, we became very much aware of all the pain in the world. Again, Helen was struck with the overwhelming realization: "I'm not just a number to God. He knows my pain. He knows what we have been struggling with."

Friends and relatives testify to the miracle we received. For example, when our neighbor across the street saw me, he said, "I don't know what happened, but you look like you're ten years younger, Brother."

Our home church pastor said, "I knew you were different the minute you walked through the door."

Helen and I praise the Lord that I have had no relapses of any kind since then! It's been nine years since God healed me.

I continued with follow-up visits to my neurologist at UNC. He is of the Jewish faith, and he was very excited when I told him what had happened. He told the nurses; everyone he saw. I continued to see him for two years. Dr. Kahn said, "There is no known cure for MS. And as a scientist, I cannot write in your medical report that you are cured [because there is no cure]. The only thing I can do is write that you are free of all symptoms. And for a man of your age, that is unheard of!" Then he added, "There is no scientific explanation for why you are symptom-free."

Now, where do we go from here?

Since that marvelous day, we have been trying to tell people that God is still doing miracles today, and we share the story of my healing. However, we have learned that some people don't want to hear it. It messes with their theology. Our goal is to teach. The Bible calls us to be followers of Christ. So that is our goal.

I can remember, early on, people would say, "You are going to have a great healing ministry. Freely you have received, so freely you will give. It's just a forgone conclusion; that's what God wants you to do."

God is sovereign, not me. God has a plan for everybody's life. As modern Americans, we have a hard time accepting this. We want to take charge. We want to make God bend to our will: "I'm going to be healed. I'm going to be wealthy. I'm not going to have any problems. Any adversity that comes my way must be an attack from the devil," and so on. In the New Testament, Paul writes about these things — adversity is a way to strengthen us; to build character; to make us even more like Christ! So we try to share these things. But again, they are usually not well received. People want to hear that God wants them to have that new bass boat, or to have that big screen TV, or to be healed of diabetes so that they can eat all the donuts they want. That is the essence of some Christians' faith.

Faith is trust; trusting God. Our plan for the future is to spread the fact — the message — that God is sovereign, not us.

Yes, you are going to have adversity. Look at Job. He is one of my personal heroes. He lost everything. I kind of lost everything. My child didn't die, but my hopes and my dreams — everything I had built up financially — are all gone. Job trusted God. He had questions, but in the midst of it all, Job's friends told him, "You brought this on yourself. You must be a horrible sinner. You deserve what happened to you. You need to repent right away and get right with God." God ends up rebuking these guys, and basically says, "You need to go to your friend, Job, and he'll pray for you. Then I will forgive you." (So Job did.)

Like Job, it's okay to question. It's possible to ask questions without losing faith.

I will be forever grateful for the amazing miracle Jesus Christ did for me. Jesus did not do this miracle for me based on any kind of personal merit. I didn't earn it or deserve it in any way. I was born deserving destruction and the hellfire of eternal damnation. And yet, my Lord Jesus had mercy on me, anyway. Not only did He heal me, He was scourged bloody in my place. He was crucified as punishment for my sin; cruelly executed for crimes I committed. He died, was buried, and came alive on the third day. He is very much alive today and forever. Right now, He is seated at God the Father's right hand. In a little while, He will return to judge the living and the dead.

You can't escape hell's lake of fire by any good work you can do. The good news is that Jesus died for you, too. You can only have eternal life by turning away from your sins and believing in Jesus Christ. Your debt has been paid and canceled by Him.

Please put your faith in Jesus.

The Story of
Timothy Carden

After longing and praying for a child for four years, and after having experienced two miscarriages, the Cardens were elated that Elaine was finally pregnant again. It was the 1980s. The doctor calculated the baby would be born in February. Imagine the anxiety they felt when Elaine began having labor pains in October! They wondered if their baby born fourteen weeks premature could possibly survive.

These lines are excerpts from Elaine Carden's diary...And a few of Timmy's early thoughts. Maybe this is how her unborn child would testify...that is if he could talk.

DAY 1

At about 10 p.m. I started having lower back pains, which I thought was to be expected at that stage of my pregnancy. The next day, about 12:30 p.m., my pains increased and I felt stomach contractions. Ryall called Dr. McNinch who told us to go to the hospital. I was examined at Prince George's Hospital (Maryland) and taken to the labor room where I was given medication (through an IV) to stop the labor.

Hey, what's happening? I'm feeling confused, and I'm scared!

During these hours, Ryall and I prayed and he read scripture to me. The labor stopped for a few hours, but then I started having heavy contractions. Doctors said the labor couldn't be stopped, and the baby's chance of survival was only twenty-five percent!

My Daddy in heaven has another plan. I know He does.

Timothy was born alive at 5:45 p.m., the next day. He weighed one pound and 11 ounces. Praise the Lord! All his body parts were there, and our hearts rejoiced. I was tired, but very thankful.

Me too!

He was taken to Baltimore City Hospital (now Johns Hopkins) which was about an hour's drive from our home in Bowie, Maryland. Troy Smith and Ryall were there, hoping to see him for the first time. Because Troy was not immediate family, he was not able to see Timothy.

DAY 3

Today I cried a lot because my son was in Baltimore and my arms were empty. I was able to come home, and received many calls and prayers for Timmy.

DAY 4

I saw my baby again — the first time since his birth. I just love the little guy so much. We couldn't hold him because of his size and because he was on a respirator. I hated to leave him there. My heart aches for him.

DAY 5

Linda, his nurse, explained that the respirator was managing/controlling his breathing 28% of the time. He weighed 1 lb., 8 oz., and his blood gases had shifted. My heart hurts at every weight-loss or change that is not positive. I pray daily for strength according to Isaiah 40:31, "But they that wait upon the Lord shall renew their strength; they shall mount up with wings as eagles; they shall run, and not be weary; and they shall walk, and not faint."

I know that's right!

DAY 6

At 5:45 a.m., we received a call from the hospital telling us that Timothy was bleeding in his lungs and may not survive. Again, my heart felt like it was being torn apart. We called Kim Cannon (our teacher and pastor) and he accompanied us to the hospital. Marla Purvis was here and made phone calls to various people to pray for our precious son.

I hope they call Doctor Jesus.

By the time we arrived at the hospital with prayer on our lips, Timmy had stabilized, and was just as active as the last time we had seen him. I must add, here, that Ryall (my wonderful strong husband) said from the start, "This is just a minor setback." God is faithful, and I must learn to trust and rely on Him more. I have claimed Psalm 37:4, 5 and 7a, among other scriptures, for my Lord's promises and strength.

"Delight thyself also in the Lord; and he shall give thee the desires of thine heart. Commit thy way unto the Lord; trust also in him; and he shall bring it to pass. Rest in the Lord and wait patiently for him."

A sonogram showed that Timmy also had some bleeding in his head, but this did not indicate brain damage or retardation. Our Christian friends have been a wonderful support to us — prayerfully and materially. We praise God for each one of them.

Timmy's respirations have been slowly improving. We praise God that he survived this crisis. Isaiah 65:24, "And it shall come to pass, that before they call, I will answer; and while they are yet speaking, I will hear."

Does Jesus hear me, too?

DAY 7

Since Timmy was affected by a temporary condition of jaundice, they began treating him with phototherapy, last night. Jaundice is very common in newborn infants. Phototherapy is a light treatment that eliminates bilirubin in the blood, and they put tape over the baby's eyelids to protect his eyes from the bright lights.

Timmy was at 50% respirator; still stable and active. When we saw Timmy on Wednesday evening, he looked thinner to me, but he was really active. We rubbed him on his hands, legs and head. I believe he knew his dad and mom were there. It still hurts my heart to leave him. I have so many tears, these days.

Please don't cry, Mommy. I know you are here. I know Daddy is here. I love hearing your voices. Please hold my hands again.

DAY 8

Timmy is one week old, today, and his nurse, Debbie, said he is doing really well — down to 38% respirator (that means he is breathing 62% on his own) and weighing 1 lb., 8 oz. He is resting on his tummy for the first time.

I like being on my tummy.

I choose to believe his progress today is because his parents visited him the night before. But tonight he lost 1/2 oz., and I was so upset I had to take a sleeping pill.

DAY 9

We visited Timmy, tonight. They were giving him blood, and his head was turned so that we couldn't see his face. Although his weight was back up to 1 lb and 8 oz, the doctor gave us a grim report and said Timmy's condition was still critical.

I'm trying, Mommy!

DAY 10

Timmy is stable, and still weighed-in at 1 lb., 8 oz. He is breathing better — respirator is down to 23%.The bilirubin was up a little, so he is still on phototherapy. I really pray that he can come off those lights soon. I think they make him perspire and lose weight and fluid.

DAY 11

Hallelujah! Timmy was taken off the phototherapy, this afternoon, so they removed the tape that covered his eyes. He is so precious. He opened his eyes, from time to time, and although I'm not sure he can hear us through the glass isolette, we talked to him a lot, today. Flora is his nurse, and she is a very sweet person from Africa. She taped a picture of an elephant on his isolette — compliments of Africa.

Even the doctor of doom, Dr. E., was more positive, today. He said Timmy's a fighter, and he was pleased with his progress.

I left the hospital with smiles, not tears.

DAY 14

They are adding more calories to his IV. Vital signs are all good. We had a really good visit. Flora let me feed Timmy through the tube. He had five feedings, today, and all has been digested well.

DAY 15

Today Timmy will be two weeks old. My sweetheart is active this morning, and — praise God — they put him on breast milk (2 cc every 2 hours). IV is still in.

Look, Mommy, no respirator!

Wow! He is breathing room air today.

DAY 16

My honeybunny is still on room air, and they increased his milk intake to 2 1/2 cc every two hours. He still has the IV, and will until he is on about 8 cc of milk. We saw him, this evening. He looked real good! His monitor showed his heart rate increasing, and the nurse said that meant he was excited by our playing and talking to him. He opened his eyes, off and on, and we had a really good visit!

I don't have a clue what they're saying to me, but I know those lovely voices.

DAY 17

All is well, and now he is getting 3 cc of breast milk every 2 hours.

Thank you, Lord Jesus!

DAY 18

I was overjoyed when I got to hold and feed Timmy, today. But after awhile he began to lose color, and his heart rate dropped. The doctor determined it was because his respirator tube had loosened so much that it might have gagged him. New tubing was put in, and my honey's color returned.

DAY 19

Timmy gained 2 oz. He now weighs 1 lb. 10 1/2 oz. Milk intake is 4 cc every 2 hours. He was doing well, this evening. Ryall was elected deacon at Riverdale Baptist tonight.

DAY 20

Timmy's color is not too good, so they put him on the respirator again at 50% oxygen, and they gave him 8cc of blood, this evening. I still have a cold, so I will not be going to see Timmy until my cold is gone. Oh, how I miss him! It feels like two steps forward; three steps back.

I miss you too, Mommy.

NOVEMBER 10 -15

I hadn't seen my baby for several days. Oh Lord Jesus, please comfort his little heart during my absence. Thank God, I could talk to the nurses by telephone — sometimes twice a day. Good reports one day…and negative reports the next. They had to give him antibiotics in case of a possible lung or blood infection. They also did a chest x-ray which indicated his lungs were not as healthy as before. He remained on the respirator at 50 - 60% oxygen. Any slightly negative report breaks my heart. We had to sign a PKU consent form for blood work for Timmy. This is a standard test to identify allergies that could cause retardation for babies.

I am praying the Lord will bring us through this. Not seeing Timmy since last Sunday had made me an extremely weepy mother. I couldn't wait to see him.

We saw him this afternoon, and got to stay quite a while. He looked like he had grown a bit. I phoned again at 9:30 p.m., and the nurse said everything was fine. God is good!

All the time!

NOVEMBER 16-20

Ryall and I both had a chance to hold our precious one tonight. We just love him so! We talked to a city doctor today. As most city doctors do, she gives you the "bad news" with both barrels. I really appreciate Ryall 'cause he can sift through the conversation better than I. Here is what it boiled down to: Timmy has to stay on high oxygen levels until his lungs grow a lot more. That will take time.

Dixie Nemeth baked a cake for Timmy's 4-week birthday, and the Cory Seniors gave him a teddy bear.

Dr. Goodman, a Johns Hopkins doctor, talked to me about the x-ray report. It shows chronic lung changes, so they will begin adding Portagen 40 to his breast milk. This will give him the calcium and calories that premature babies need.

NOVEMBER 21

Tiny Tim is gaining weight! Today he weighed 1 lb and 12 oz. — the highest he's been yet! He was on 70% oxygen, 26 breaths per minute. All is well. We only held him for a few minutes today.

NOVEMBER 23

The last few days have been full of drama — first good news, then bad. We go to see him every day, and my emotions have been on a roller coaster. It's amazing the things these babies go through, and sometimes the parents aren't told until after the fact. I guess if we really knew all the details it would tear at our hearts even more.

Mommy, Daddy: Your strength comes from Jesus, and my strength comes from you!

NOVEMBER 24

Dr. G. said Timmy has made a lot of progress this month. He now weighs 1 lb.,13 oz. He had his eyes open a lot, and we were able to hold him for a little while. What a joy!

NOVEMBER 26

Timmy met his grandparents today. My mom and dad were seeing him for the first time, and we all took pictures. He kept looking at me, this afternoon, as I held him. What a doll! Tonight, when I called, his nurse said he was resting well. She reminded me to bring in some milk.

No canned milk, please. I like your milk, Mom!

DECEMBER 3

Praise the Lord! Six days have gone by with nothing unusual to report. Timmy now weighs 2 lbs, 2 oz., and he has been very active; so much so, he pulled his respirator tube out, again. The nurse let me hold him for a little while.

DECEMBER 7

When we saw Timmy, tonight, he looked even bigger. He is still gaining — now up to 2 lbs, 4 oz. The nurse has increased his feedings, and praise God, all his vital signs are good!

DECEMBER 8

Tiny Tim is growing — now weighs in at 2 lbs, 5 3/4 oz.

DECEMBER 9

I held him for two hours this afternoon. I love him so much! I kissed him and sang to him. I really enjoyed my visit, this afternoon, and I hope Timmy did, too.

Every minute of it, Mommy!

DECEMBER 13

This kid is growing by leaps and bounds — gained 3 ounces since December 8. His daddy held him tonight, and we sang duets to him. He was looking around a lot, and his eyes were so bright. The nurse took pictures of him. He is so cute!!! We will go to the annual Pastor's Banquet tomorrow night and show pictures of him to anyone who'll look. So many friends in church have been praying for him.

DECEMBER 16-21

Timmy sure doesn't like that respirator. He pulled out his tube four times on December 16.

At first I wasn't strong enough to fight that mean, old plastic tube. Now I am!

For the next five days, he extubated so much they had to stitch the tube to his lip so he could not pull it out. Dr. Cringer said they did this because intubating him so much could affect his vocal cords. If this doesn't work, they will have to sedate him. A lot of negative stuff is happening, these last few days, and it sure keeps us on our knees.

Dr. Crissinger called after 11 p.m., one night, to let us know Timmy was doing better. As she was calling, I was praying for our son. Praise God! He answered before we finished asking Him. (Isaiah 65:24, "And it shall come to pass, that before they call, I will answer; and while they are yet speaking, I will hear.")

They took another sonogram on December 20, and there was no indication of bleeding at all. Praise the Lord for answering our prayers!

DECEMBER 25

Thank God for a great Christmas present — all Timothy's vitals are good, today, and he weighs 3 lb. We took pictures of Timmy wearing a

Santa Claus hat, a gift from our friend, Dixie Nemeth. I held him awhile, and Ryall played with him. Later we had dinner with the Donbergers. It was a wonderful Christmas.

Happy Birthday, Lord Jesus! But who is Santa Claus?

JANUARY 1

Although there were complications, Timmy's parents were confident the worst was over by this time. Now he was gaining weight regularly, and his vital signs were usually good. All the nurses loved the little guy, and the Johns Hopkins doctors were dedicated and persistent!

Happy New Year, everybody!

Epilogue

The Cardens continued visiting Timmy in the hospital nearly every day until they took him home six weeks later.

It is a real pleasure to meet Timothy Carden. The miracle baby grew up to be a big, strong, handsome man with a contagious smile. He did very well in school. Honor Roll at Annapolis Area Christian High, and he made the Dean's List at both Anne Arundel Community College and Bowie State University (BSU). He obtained an Associate of Science degree in Business Administration at AACC, and a Bachelor of Science degree at BSU. He enjoys his position as Management and Program Analyst for the U.S. Department of Justice.

Tim loves to talk about his miraculous infancy, and uses his story as a witnessing tool for our Lord Jesus. He says, "More than anything, I want my life to be a testimony to the power and love of God."

I believe he is living up to his name. Timothy means "Honoring God."

The Story of
Neila Oberg Arouca
As written by Neila

It was spring, 2002. I was finishing my freshman year at Southwestern Adventist University in Keene, Texas. I was far from home. It had been a little over a year since I had left Brazil to study in the U.S. I had always been very true to my faith, but there was something about coming to a different country and experiencing a new freedom that seemed to distract me from God.

One morning near the end of spring semester, I woke up with large bruises on my legs. A few days before, while walking home with friends, I'd tripped and fallen. I had expected to see some bruises, but that morning I discovered about five or six large bruises on my legs. This seemed very strange, and — feeling that I needed my mother's advice — I called home. Mom thought it seemed normal because I had recently fallen; she told me I shouldn't worry about it. My Father in heaven knew differently. God knew that the bruises meant something else and that they should be addressed. So later that day, He arranged for me to chat with my grandma and tell her about the unusual bruises. Since Grandma had recently dealt with a family member diagnosed with internal bleeding, she was especially interested in other symptoms I was having. From the symptoms I described, she warned my mom that my situation could be more serious than she'd thought, and that I should get checked by a doctor.

That afternoon, I got a phone call from my mom and dad. They said that I should go to the hospital just to make sure the bruising and symptoms weren't serious. At the time, I didn't have a car. So I decided to go to the college nurse and arrange an appointment with a physician later that week. My parents were not satisfied, though, and knowing that it would be difficult to convince me to go to the emergency room for bruises, they managed to find an English-speaking friend (in Brazil) to call the girls' dean and ask her to check on me; to take me to a doctor. It may sound like they were being over-protective, but God knew I didn't have much time. He was working on their hearts.

My parents' friend was trying to explain who I was to the receptionist at the ladies' dorm, but since I lived off-campus she didn't know how to help. As they were talking on the phone, David Knight (who was Dean of Student Affairs at the time) walked into the lobby, overheard the receptionist's conversation, and intervened. He told my parents not to worry because he would take me to the hospital. (Later, he told my parents and me that he had just finished his work for that day, and was about to go home. But God impressed upon him to make a stop at the ladies' dorm just to be sure everything was okay. God works in marvelous ways!)

The sun had almost set when I got a phone call from Dean Knight saying that he would be coming by to take me to the doctor. He took me to their family physician, who said it could be serious and even mentioned leukemia. My next stop was the emergency room. The doctor examined me and ordered an abdominal CAT scan, right away. As I had expected, he said that the bruises did not concern him very much, but something else — something that I wasn't even paying much attention to — did! The doctor pointed out that I had tiny red dots all over my body. He told me that they were little blood vessels that were rupturing. I lay in the ER bed thinking about how fast everything was happening, trying not to be anxious as I waited. My loved ones were so far away!

After the laboratory results came through, the doctor returned with a better — but more complicated — term than leukemia: Idiopathic Thrombocytopenic Purpura, or ITP. It was better because, unlike leukemia, ITP is an immune system disorder that kills platelets instead of failing to produce them. (A not-so-pleasant bone marrow biopsy confirmed that my body was producing platelets.) For unknown reasons, my body decided that my platelets were intruders, and set out to destroy them. Platelets are responsible for coagulation, without which I could literally bleed to death. My platelet count — that night in the emergency room — was around 15,000/uL, which is very low compared to a normal count that ranges from 150,000 to 450,000/uL. I was then admitted to a hospital bed. All the attention I was getting felt very strange. It was hard getting used to the idea that I was seriously ill.

Within hours, my parents had received a call with the updated details. They decided that Mom would fly to Texas as soon as she could. When all arrangements have been made in advance, travel from Brazil is easy. But for my mom (who had no passport, no visa, no plane ticket, no packed bags, and a sick daughter in a hospital 5,000 miles away) things could prove to be quite difficult. Pulling all the documentation together could have significantly delayed her, but God is the Creator of time, and miracles started to happen right away. It was 9:00 a.m. when she left her workplace. By 3:30 p.m., she was sitting at the airport with everything in hand — passport, visa and plane tickets!

Back in Texas, I got a visit from a doctor who explained ITP in more detail. The doctor told me that the disorder is usually found in older people (in a chronic way) or in young children (in an acute way). I didn't fit into either category very well. Mine was apparently acute, but in a more chronic way.

My mom arrived the next morning. The doctor prescribed strong doses of cortisone, hoping to weaken my immune system. The plan of care didn't work. I had a strong immune system and it simply wouldn't weaken.

Later that month, the doctor decided to treat me with intravenous immunoglobulin (which contains plasma) in an attempt to decrease the severity of my disorder. This treatment is normally administered monthly, but in my case, it had to be done weekly. Unfortunately, my platelet counts would only increase the first day of treatment, and then drop again. For almost three months I continued with outpatient immunoglobulin therapy.

It was summertime, the campus was almost barren, and I couldn't fly to Brazil because of my delicate condition. I was stuck, but I was where God wanted me to be, and being stuck was good for my faith. During that time, I had plenty of time to think things over, look at my life, get closer to God, and learn to completely depend upon His love.

My mom used to say that I was like glass — so fragile that I couldn't afford to fall, be hit, or get cut anywhere. To bleed was something I could not afford. Unfortunately, the doctor and I had forgotten about menstruation, and one day I woke up with a hemorrhage that couldn't be stopped. It lasted 24 days. I became anemic. On one occasion, during that time, I complained to Mom that I felt very dizzy, and my feet and hands were numb. She rushed me to the hospital, but there was nothing they could do — no medicine; no surgery. The doctors said that we could only wait for my body to respond. We knew only God could help us, so Mom called home and asked the family to pray. God responded quickly. In a short while, the bleeding stopped. God was there the whole time, miracle after miracle!

During that summer, Pastor Ron Halvorsen, Jr., and Dean David Knight came to talk with me about being anointed. They explained to me that according to James 5:14, it would mean that I would place my life in God's hands and ask Him to heal me. I wanted God to heal me, so I decided to place my life in His hands, ask for His will to be done, and accept the anointing.

After ten treatments of immunoglobulin, there had been no positive response from my body, so the doctor decided on a more aggressive approach. He told me that the next step was to do a splenectomy. In other words, they would surgically remove my spleen. If that were to happen, I would have to live the rest of my life taking vaccines to compensate for the loss of my spleen. The vaccines are not so bad, and a lot of people live like that. But to me, removing my spleen meant that I was giving up on God's power to heal. I knew He could heal me, and I knew He had given me a spleen for a reason. I was sure that it was His will that I should keep it. In addition, I was a young woman. Privately, I couldn't stop thinking about the scar the surgery would leave on my body. I did not want that scar, but I didn't tell anyone about this. Only God could read my thoughts.

The day of the surgery was approaching, and there was still no improvement in my health. My mom always says that God usually works at the last minute because this shows us that it was not possible for a human being to have done it. I had faith, and I was waiting for God's perfect timing. A few days before the surgery, the doctor began giving me more doses of immunoglobulin to prepare me for surgery. The splenectomy only offered a 50 percent chance of cure. There was the possibility that, after my spleen was removed, another organ (like the liver, for example) would resume the spleen's job. This would send me back to square one.

Remarkably, my body started to respond very well to the pre-operative immunoglobulin shots, and my platelet level increased. I told my doctor that I didn't want to go through with the surgery because God was healing me, but the doctor said that it was only the pre-operative medicine that had caused the change. He insisted that I should have the surgery.

That night, God revealed something that meant a lot to me. Through a family member, God showed me that it was not His will that I should have a permanent scar on my tummy. Only God and I had known about that scar issue. How could it be that this loved one was virtually speaking my thoughts? Then I knew that God was telling me that He didn't want that scar on me, either. I felt so happy! I knew He was going to heal me.

A day before the surgery, I went to see the surgeon for my pre-op evaluation. My platelet level had increased, and I told him that I felt in my heart that I should not go through with that surgery. He warned me that it was a dangerous decision, but acknowledged that I was free to choose. So, I chose to give it to God; I trusted Him.

The next day, the day that I was supposed to be in surgery, I went to get more blood work done. It revealed that my platelet level had gone from 4,000/uL to 260,000/uL! I was so glad that I was not on that operating table having my spleen removed! The doctor was not as positive, though. He was not pleased that I had cancelled the surgery, and said the only reason I was doing so well was because of the pre-op treatment I was receiving.

About a month later, I went back to see my doctor. He was sure that my platelet count would have dropped by then, but to his surprise, it was even higher. He apologized to me, and said that my faith had saved my spleen. He also said that in his twenty-year career, he had never seen a case like mine. He had never seen a platelet level (nearing zero for nearly three months) return to normal in one day, and stay normal. God gave me a miracle! Praise His holy name! What was meant to be a curse turned out to be many blessings!

David and Juliet Knight invited me to live with their family, and theirs became my home for the remainder of my college life. They are family to me, and I am so blessed to have them in my life! It is also exciting that friends — who were praying for me — got to see for themselves that God really answers prayers. And most important of all, my faith was exercised, making it purer and stronger. I've come to know God on a personal level, which is the biggest blessing of all!

Many years later, as I was reading and meditating on Christ's sacrifice, it hit me that Jesus' hands and feet and His side carry permanent scars. My thoughts flashed back to my conversation with God that day before my scheduled surgery, and I came to the realization that Jesus chose to carry that scar in my place! I have no words to thank Him for His sacrifice and for the little and big things He did and does for me.

I love you, Jesus!

The Story of
Anita Tharasingh
& Brian Beavers

As told by Anita and Brian

ANITA: The year was 2004. It was the last week and month of the year, December 24th through the 26th. These dates have been indelibly etched in our minds, reminding us of God's loving care for His flock. Green Pastures, a little missionary training school located in a small village called Temple in the Wilderness, was off for a long weekend to the Scripture Union campsite. The lovely spot is located on the second longest coastline in the country, Mahabalipuram, Madras, Tamil Nadu in South India.

The idea to travel there was born as Timothy and I were celebrating our twenty-fifth wedding anniversary on December 27. Our children, Tania and Brian, were married in June of that year. The children at our school and orphanage had never seen the sea or experienced being at the beach, so we decided to spend that special window of time with family and our school children — all eighteen remaining at the school for the holidays.

We arrived by train on Friday, from Mumbai, and taxied to the beach. After introductions to other Seventh-day Adventist members from nearby Christian Medical College, we had wonderful fellowship, sharing and singing for vespers, outdoors. Our friends told us that they would be staying at the campus for the weekend, and we already knew most of the young college students and staff. There was much excitement as we made plans for Sabbath services, etc. December 25th, Sabbath morning, found us all in a small hall, deeply engrossed, studying the book of "Daniel and Revelation," and Brian Beavers (our son-in-law) was leading in Sabbath School.

Later, after a short break, we all gathered in the garden area under the casuarina trees, sat on benches in a circle, and listened to the sermon from one of the elders, contemplating the goodness of our Lord. Our school children who are, for the most part, from northeast India, sang for us in their native tongues (Hindi, Bodo, and Assamese). All appreciated the fervor and zeal of these kids, and many were inspired by the words in the Christian songs.

After closing the Sabbath and partaking of a small supper, we all walked on the beach. It was a brilliantly moonlit night. As we got better acquainted with the other group of believers, there was peace, joy and happiness all around. While the rest of the world celebrated Christmas with some drinking, carousing, and other festivities, His children were praising the Creator of the universe. Little did we know what was brewing in the Indonesian Islands on the other side of the Bay of Bengal. For some reason, my husband was not on the beach with us, as he was compelled to fast and pray.

Sunday morning, December 26 found us on the beach, well into our morning worship. As we watched the sunrise and drank in the beauty of the ocean and rolling waves, it made us aware of His presence and marvel at His love for mankind. The thought for the day, the Lord put in my heart that morning, was taken from Job 38:8-11. Verse 11 says, "And hitherto shalt thou come, but no further; and here shall thy proud waves be stayed?" I was always very wary about the waves of the ocean, since they are unpredictable, so I never ventured anywhere close. But somehow that morning, I claimed God's protection, and (together with the little ones) we went to play at the edge of the water. The older boys, who knew how to swim, were walking into the sea. So I let them, with a gentle reminder to keep within limits, as the waves appeared to be boisterous.

After a half hour of romping and rollicking in the sand and surf, some of them were collecting shells and were in no mood to return. However, as it was getting close to breakfast time, we were asked to get to our rooms to shower and be ready as soon as possible. After two more frantic calls from my husband, we finally wrenched ourselves from the beach, saying in our minds, "We'll be back."

When we got back from the seashore, we were told to move our stuff from the ground floor to the upstairs dorm rooms, where the children and workers were housed. This was to make room for incoming guests who urgently needed our rooms. Brian and Tania moved their luggage, laptop and projector, which Brian used extensively to give Power Point presentations at camp meetings. We moved our luggage, and cleared out of the ground floor. Not until later did we realize God's awesome hand in all of this sudden change in plans. Sometimes, what seems like a little inconvenience is God's way of shielding us from something terrible.

All showered and dressed, we piled into the hired minibus that took us from the campsite to a vegetarian restaurant on the opposite side of the road. It was now about 8:30 a.m., and we were all happy to enjoy our breakfast. Once that was done, as we were filing out of the restaurant, we heard someone frantically cry, "The ocean has come out! The ocean has come out!" We did not fully fathom the impact of those words; not until the bus turned in at the gated driveway. There was water all over the grounds. The place seemed deserted as the older boys bounded to the ground floor of the building they had occupied the night before. To their utter amazement and disbelief, they saw the whole place covered in water, seaweed, fish, mud, and debris. Huge cupboards and desks were toppled over, and all their stuff was floating on the water — shoes, clothes, mats, etc. They picked up their belongings and made for the door, as the security guards were warning us to evacuate. It was dangerous, they said. Tidal waves were hitting the shoreline. The waves, some thirty to forty feet high, and incredibly strong winds were tearing down things along their path. Walls lay in heaps; trees were uprooted; men, women and children...were swept away into the ocean. Some had been tossed up in the air and were caught between branches, or were hanging from them. It was terrifying.

Meanwhile, the women, the girls, and Tania and Brian and I ran to retrieve our stuff from the first floor of our building. I quickly stole a bird's eye view of the garden where we had worshiped on Sabbath. The place was covered, and it glistened in the morning light; the swimming pool was a mess. The water was brown with oil and sludge. While I was just wondering what could have happened to us if we'd been on the beach, the security guard tugged at my arm and ordered us to leave.

He shouted, "Another wave is coming. You will never be able to get out of the building in time if you do not leave immediately!" I thankfully grabbed my bags, and ran out the door.

As the bus pulled out of the driveway, the second wave chased us off the campgrounds.

Fleeing as quickly as we could, the gap widened between our vehicle and the impending doom. When we came upon an Adventist doctor whom we recognized, we stopped. He and his wife were examining their car, which had been thrown fifty feet from where it had been parked! Since it was standing in water, it would not start. We got out to see if we could help. They told us a mechanic was already on his way, and encouraged us to get going (since there were children on the bus). We were so relieved that the Lord spared our lives and provided private transport for us to get away.

BRIAN: As we traveled, we witnessed utter despair. Hundreds of people thronged the roadside, a few possessions on their heads or under their arms. It looked apocalyptic, like the time of trouble described in Bible prophecy. I began to talk to the Lord and ask Him many questions: "What happened? How did it happen? Oh Lord, why did You save me?"

The Lord provides — in a still, small voice — the answer to my last question, "Because of a promise you made to Me several years ago — to serve Me for the rest of your life."

Tears rolled down my cheeks as I realized and absorbed the intensity of God's love for me.

In the evening, myself and two secondary school students — Joab and Jonah, were scheduled to travel by train to the week-long All India All African Student Association (AIAASA) Southern Zone camp meeting in Madurai. Because the tracks were covered in Madras (Chennai) we drove more than forty-five minutes out of the way to catch our train. God not only preserved our seats — a real miracle in India — He also gave us the privilege of preparing ten to twelve students to give their lives to the Lord in the waters of baptism. I am still only beginning to understand God's amazing plan for my life.

God has a wonderful plan for everyone. All He asks from us is surrender. When you surrender to Him and dedicate your life to His service, all of Heaven is at your disposal!

The Story of
Ron Baule

As told by Ron's sister (Betty Priddy),
Betty's husband (Jim Priddy) and Ron

BETTY: My son Jimmy burst into my bedroom about 11 p.m. on Sunday night. "Mom, wake up! Someone from church just called me. Uncle Ron's been in a bad accident." While they were driving home from church, a drunken driver hit them head-on. Ron, his wife, and Matthew were all badly hurt."

I begged for more details.

"They've been taken to Calvert Memorial Hospital in Prince Frederick — I'm sorry, Mom. That's all they would tell me," Jimmy said.

I jumped in the car and raced over there. The hospital is about seventeen miles from our home in Lusby, Maryland. When I arrived at Calvert Memorial, a nurse told me that Ronnie's body had been starved of oxygen for sixteen minutes; the accident had made his heart stop beating. Since he had obviously passed, he'd been flown to Southern Maryland Hospital in Clinton — D.O.A. (dead on arrival). Ron had been in the Coast Guard, so they'd transported his body in a Patuxent Naval Air helicopter. It was at Southern Maryland Hospital that God showed His hand.

JIM: It happened about 9:30 p.m. on June 6, 1986, on Rosby Hall Road in the Lusby area just about six miles from his home. A passing motorist called 911, and MEDSTAR was contacted.

Medics pulled Ron's bleeding body out of a mangled pile of broken glass and steel but his heart had stopped beating. From all appearances, Ron was dead!

First, they took Jackie and Matthew (Ron's wife and four-year-old son) to Calvert Memorial in Prince Frederick. They were both in the ICU. Doctors were working on Jackie, who was suffering with serious internal injuries and a broken foot. Poor little Matthew could not stop crying until I held him in my arms. His legs were broken, but they hadn't had time to work on him yet.

RON: After the accident, I was sitting in the car. I felt supernaturally peaceful. No pain; no worries; content to be dead; just resting in the Lord's arms. Suddenly, God — or perhaps it was an angel — spoke to me, saying: "Ronnie, wake up. Satan was after you." I heard from God, and woke up. A doctor heard me groan, and he shouted, "Oh my God, my God! He's alive! Get him over to Washington Hospital Center right away!"

JIM: Betty called me about 1:00 a.m. to say Ron was alive and they'd taken him by Air Evac to Washington Hospital Center (WHC). Our oldest son, Jimmy, went with me. When we arrived at WHC, they were taking Ron to surgery. This was about 4:30 a.m., so at least seven hours had lapsed since the accident. The doctors met me in the hallway. I walked alongside Ron's gurney. His whole face was smashed in, and the doctor told me he only had a two percent chance of survival. I asked if I could pray for him. The doctor said, "Better make it quick." I didn't know what to pray. I thought, "How can I pray for a dead person?" So right there in the elevator, I prayed in the Spirit prayed in tongues. We went back downstairs to the waiting room, and we were there until about 2 o'clock in the afternoon.

The chaplain — a young student from some nearby theological seminary — was there with me.

After talking with him for awhile, I could see that he wasn't born again. He asked me, "What was that language you were praying in?"

I told him, "I really didn't know how to pray, and I don't know what I said, but I knew if I prayed in the Spirit, God would touch him." Then I started telling the intern about Jesus, and prayed with him to receive the Lord. Before he went off duty at about eight o'clock, he said, "Man, I am sure glad I stopped in here and had the chance to talk to you."

BETTY: When I arrived at WHC, I was taken to the ICU where I saw a policeman who looked familiar. I approached him, and he told me the guy who hit Ron was drunk as a skunk, and driving about 90 miles per hour. He was in a bed in the cubicle next to us, and we could hear him bawling, "SHOOT ME! SHOOT ME! PLEASE SOME-BODY SHOOT ME!"

I screamed, "If I had a gun, I would gladly shoot you!"

I was beside myself with rage, and was ready to say a lot more...until I distinctly heard the voice of God speak to me, "If it were not for my grace, your father, who had once been a drunken driver, would have been shot." God gave me the peace and strength to truly forgive that miserable drunk. All the anger and bitterness simply drained out of me. God is so good.

Back when I'd learned to hear God's voice, I had asked the Lord, "Lord, how can I be sure that I am hearing Your voice, and it's not my own voice?"

The Lord replied, "Because there is nothing good in you, except for Me."

The next three days in the waiting room were probably the longest days in my life — just waiting to see Ron. We spent most of the time just crying out to God. "Please don't let my brother die!"

My friend, a little Catholic lady named Stella, said, "I went to see him every day and rebuked the spirit of death."

I thought about his life up to now. He had enjoyed such a rich life, and was a blessing to everyone. Ron joined the Coast Guard in 1967. Since he had natural mechanical abilities and was skilled at working with numbers, he enjoyed his duties as a machinist mate. He left the Coast Guard in 1981, and built a very successful career as an engineer with several big, oil-drilling companies in China, Brazil, Indonesia, Saudi Arabia, and India.

Ron loved the Lord, and he and our whole family were Spirit-filled Christians, and members of the Full Gospel Business Men's Fellowship International. Ron was a strong witness for Jesus wherever he went, and on his last day in India, he led thirteen men to the Lord. The next day, he came back home and immediately started part time work for a realtor. Two of the owners had not gone to church for over a year, but Ron persuaded them to attend church again.

JIM: When we finally got to see Ron (three days after the accident) he looked like he weighed about 450 pounds. His head was swollen-up larger than a basketball; his body was filled with fluid; his legs were smashed and swollen—looked like big balloons! But, praise God...he was alive! His mangled body looked so terrible, when we took Matthew to see him, he couldn't bear to look at his dad.

He was in a coma for seventy-eight days. When he first came out of the coma, he didn't even know us. He had lost his sense of reason, and Satan took advantage of this. Although he'd never been one to cuss, after the accident he cussed constantly.

He was in a wheelchair for a long time. The doctor said that Ron would never be able to walk again. But Doctor Jesus knew better. The Great Physician said, "It's not how much scripture you know," and "It doesn't depend on your faith. It all depends on My faith." Soon after that, Ron began walking with a cane.

One day we all went to a healing service in Lancaster, California. The preacher laid hands on Ron and commanded the demons to leave in the name of Jesus. Ron fell down as seven demons left him. When the evil spirits hit the road, their profanity went with them, and like canes and crutches never came back! Two minutes later, without canes or crutches, Ron stood up and walked out of that gym, and 1/4 mile farther to his car. Hallelujah!

Epilogue

Ron Baule is once again a powerful and faithful witness for our Lord Jesus Christ. At age 63, he looks great physically strong and healthy. Other than having a minor problem with his eyesight near the end of the day, he is unimpaired when he occasionally helps friends with construction jobs. Ron will be forever grateful that a "two percent chance" was plenty for Doctor Jesus!

The Story of
Brenda Russell

As told by Brenda

In late April 1999, I woke up in the middle of the night and noticed a lump just above my collarbone. *Strange*, I thought. I made a mental note, and went back to sleep. I was exhausted. In the morning, I rolled out of bed and headed straight for the mirror. I couldn't see a lump, so using the pads of my fingers, I explored my neck and shoulder. Sure enough, it was there. "I think I'll make an appointment with my doctor to get this checked out," I told my husband. My comment surprised Freddie — knows me well. My usual approach to illness is to self-diagnose and self-treat.

Freddie is known as "Pastor Russell" to thousands. To this day, the fact that I am "Mrs. Freddie Russell" baffles me, at times. As a young woman, I had made a list of professionals that I did not want to marry. "Pastor" was at the top! I am the oldest of three children, and the two younger ones were already married. So when I accepted Freddie's proposal, it should have been no surprise to me that my dearest Friend approached me with a critical question, "Why do you want to marry him?"

God really does know best. It was His Spirit — my dearest Friend — asking me this question. In asking me *why*, the Lord was drawing to my attention the trust issue, wanting me to think long and hard about trusting Him; trusting His guidance. I also believe God was asking me to examine my reasons for wanting to be married. Did I really love Freddie, or was I just getting married to keep up with my siblings and get the old church ladies off my back? I think the Lord wanted me to be sure that I was ready to be joined to a minister. Though we all have a direct responsibility to God, people look to pastors for strong leadership. Until this point — the point where I heard God's voice ask the question — I hadn't really thought about what my responsibility as a pastor's wife would entail. Did I really love God enough to commit my life to the new lifestyle I was about to embrace? Looking back, I praise God for leading me to self-examine. I praise Him for bringing my husband and me together. I praise Him for speaking to me that day, because it was this experience that allowed me to recognize His voice the next time.

Two days had passed since I first felt the lump. Now I found myself sitting across from my doctor, a bit shell-shocked from having answered a boatload of questions. "You know, we could be looking at cancer, here," he said. That was the last thing I expected to hear. He explained that he would run me through a series of tests, starting with a chest x-ray, some blood-work, and a mammogram. I started the process immediately, and after a second battery of tests, my doctor sent me to a surgeon for a fine-needle biopsy. The procedure was unsuccessful, so I was sent for a surgical biopsy. Those results wouldn't be ready for me for a few days. The irony.

The results would soon be ready for me, but was I ready for them?

A whole month had passed since I first discovered the lump. I'd been poked, prodded, sliced, and scanned. I prayed for a benign diagnosis, but a benign diagnosis was not my good fortune. In the second-to-last week of May, I was told that I had Hodgkin's Disease. They were certain of the diagnosis because of the presence of Reed-Sternberg cells, even though I didn't fall into any of the categories of people who are usually stricken with Hodgkin's Disease: I am not male, not Caucasian, and was not in the right age group (neither 19 to 35 nor over 55 years of age).

Freddie and I prayed with the kids when we learned my diagnosis. We always try to keep them involved in matters that impact the whole family. We stressed that we needed to trust God in every situation in our lives. At the time, my husband was the senior pastor at the Miracle Temple Seventh-day Adventist (SDA) Church in Baltimore. I was serving as the Pathfinder Leader. Pathfinders are a club of (mostly Adventist) boys and girls ages 10 and up, who focus on memorizing and understanding God's Word; developing practical skills and a knowledge of nature; and engaging in service-related, wholesome and fun activities. Our long-awaited Memorial Day weekend camp-out was just around the corner. The timing could not have been more perfect. God knew that I would need this time away — quiet time with Him, surrounded by His beautiful creation. That weekend gave me an opportunity to absorb what I'd just been told, and to be still enough to hear God's voice. Even though my Pathfinders were inner-city kids (who ordinarily resolved to have a "mind of their own") when we were out in nature, they listened to me and obeyed my instructions. What a blessing!

I knew that there were SDA wellness centers scattered across the country. In pursuit of healing, I felt that this would be the route to take. So when my primary care physician called me, the following week, to let me know he was arranging for me to see an oncologist, he didn't capture my full attention. Nevertheless, I went to see the specialist, and listened while he explained that we needed to act quickly...that the disease was a rare form of cancer...that cancer is ravaging...that cancer does not wait.

My husband and I started calling wellness centers. Each center we called explained to us that cancer was not their forte. Since Hodgkin's Disease had a pretty high cure rate, we were advised to go through the chemotherapy, and then turn to the wellness center for reconditioning and rebuilding of the immune system.

I am no doctor, but this wasn't making sense to me. My immune system was already compromised. The way I saw it, why would I tear down my immune system (hitting rock bottom) only to turn around and try to build it back up again? What if it didn't work? So Freddie and I kept calling around. Uchee Pines (a faith-based center in Alabama) was willing to welcome me, pretreatment. But home was Maryland, and our kids Ashley and Andy were still young — ages 15 and 11. So my going to Alabama seemed far out of the question.

I was growing discouraged, and my oncologist was applying more and more pressure for me to start chemotherapy. Since things weren't panning out with the wellness centers, I reluctantly consented to chemotherapy. This would consist of treatments every other Friday, for twenty-four weeks. We sent our son to my parents because I didn't want him to see me looking the way that chemo would make me look. Our daughter had a summer job, so she remained with us.

The first treatment made me very tired and sick to my stomach. The second treatment caused a terrible bout of constipation. My body was struggling. It felt like there was fluid moving around a cement wall in the center of my body. When I talked to the oncology nurse about it, she recommended half a bottle of magnesium citrate. Despite her warnings about all the power in that little green bottle, nothing happened! So I called the nurse, and she cautiously advised me to drink the other half. Again, nothing happened! It was only after I followed the nurse's direction to take half of a second bottle that I had success. It felt like pieces of my gut had been chipped off, and my insides were blowing out. My energy was utterly drained.

By the third chemotherapy treatment, I had lost three fourths of my hair, my skin was ashen, and though I had lost only five pounds, I looked like I had lost twenty. My fingernails were fragile, I looked shriveled up and was becoming weaker. All of this...after only three treatments! I felt like I could not make it through all twelve treatments.

Because God has written His law on my heart, it is an honor to live according to His will. By the grace of Jesus Christ, I am faithful to my husband, I do not murder, I keep His Sabbath day holy, I abhor idolatry, etc. (Exodus 20.) So as I sat on my bed one Sabbath day, I worshipped my Creator and I began to pray. "God," I pleaded, "I had asked You to show me a way to be healed without having to go the route of chemo. I don't understand why You're not talking to me." Before my illness, I would pray to God, and it seemed He would answer my prayers right away. God's answers generally came in the form of other people's words or actions; or setting answers right in front of me; or, on rare occasions, I had even thought I'd heard His voice. This time, it seemed like He wasn't communicating with me at all. He was silent!

So I sat there that Sabbath, worshipping God; wrestling with my thoughts; and wrestling with Him. Then, I heard this mid-range, male voice speak. In a clear, firm but gentle voice, He asked me, "Have I ever failed you?" This was clearly the voice of authority I had heard in the past. My instant reaction was to turn my head to see who'd spoken. I was alone in the room.

"No, Lord, you haven't."

"Well," came His response, "why won't you trust Me now?"

Wow! "God, I am so sorry that I am not trusting You!"

I realized that God had not been silent. He had been sending people my way to share with me their stories, or the story of someone they knew. All along, I'd been hearing of healings "au naturel," from Hodgkin's Disease. If I had been still for a moment, I would have put the pieces together earlier. I would have been able to see how God had been sending me answers, for weeks. People had been flooding me with offers of support, encouragement, and testimonies. But I had been waiting for God to hand me a structured program; one with step-by-step directions. The wellness centers had been my mental block. They weren't giving me the answer that I'd been waiting for.

Lesson learned, I accepted God's power to make things happen. Freddie and I decided to apply to Hartland Institute in Rapidan, Virginia, since it was the closest Adventist wellness center to our home. I applied. Despite their earlier advice for me to finish the chemotherapy first, they accepted me!

Back then, health insurance companies were not very receptive to alternative medicine, so there was no chance of insurance reimbursement for participating in a wellness center program! Since we couldn't afford the twenty-one-day program, we budgeted for the ten-day. On Monday, I called my oncologist and told him about my decision. He disapproved. He did not understand what I was doing. It made no sense to him that I was choosing an option that has not been documented as a proven remedy for my illness. Chemo, on the other hand, has a documented cure rate of 85%.

I told my oncologist, "I need to trust my God. This is the direction He's taking me, so I need to go this route." He was quite upset with me. "If you were my wife," he declared, "you would not have an option!" He called my primary care physician who then called me and tried to encourage me to continue with the chemo. One or the other called me every day for a week, but to no avail. "We really want you to be able to see your kids grow up. We want you to know your grandchildren," my doctors said. "So do I," was my reply. "I have no other plan." My oncologist warned me of the grim prognosis, but I stood my ground. "I need you to know," he said, "that if you don't continue with chemo, you'll be covered from head to toe with evidence of metastatic cancer the very next time I see you.

Once he was convinced that there was no changing my mind, I asked him, "Will you still follow me?"

"Sure," my oncologist agreed. "I'll follow you. I'll start by ordering four more tests because I need to have a baseline."

These subsequent scans and blood work revealed that there was still cancer in my body. My lymph nodes on both sides of my esophagus had shrunken a little bit from the chemotherapy, but they were still visibly very large on the scan. My next appointment with the oncologist was made for November. Lord, bring on the miracle!

The Hartland staff placed me on a pre-admission protocol (which included a strictly plant-based diet; certain teas, roots, and herbs; and six garlic cloves [steamed] twice a day). I followed their instructions, precisely.

The time came for my son to return home. Unfortunately, I only then learned that while he was with my parents, he had overheard relatives expressing their doubts and frustration about my decision to stop the chemo. Finding this out months later, I was devastated! The tears just flowed. I was mortified that my baby boy had been exposed to such negative talk during such a difficult time of separation from his parents and sister. Naturally, it scared him! He feared that his mother would not be alive to greet him when he returned from North Carolina. Thank God I was!

I am convinced that serenity plays a tremendous part in healing. I arrived at Hartland Wellness Center in the middle of summer — August to be exact. Freddie stayed home with the kids while I embarked on my journey in faith. The atmosphere at Hartland was the most serene environment I had ever experienced. I was surrounded by trees, a variety of plants and fowl, a lake, and a surreal kind of peace and quiet. I'm not sure if the beauty of it all was more about my perception than about the place itself, but it doesn't matter. God used Hartland to make me whole.

The staff treated me as though I was the only guest they had. That's how they do things. In advance, they had asked for my History & Physical, as well as the results of my tests. During my Hartland assessment, I sat with a physician and a nurse to review my history and treatment plan. Several days after I arrived (and just before I left) my blood was drawn and analyzed.

I attended nutrition, wellness, and cooking classes, and was delighted to receive a cookbook with strictly plant-based recipes. Most guests' treatment plans included hydrotherapy, and each of us was given an individualized exercise program. We exercised every morning. We ate only two meals per day (intentionally) and fifty percent of our diet consisted of raw foods (i.e., foods that had not been heated to 120+ degrees). We were informed that the enzymes in uncooked foods are needed in order for the body to heal itself. Foods with added sugar were virtually eliminated. I also learned about the harmful effects of eating meat, and about the various ways in which animals are raised and fed to prepare their flesh and by-products for market.

The amazing thing about this experience is that I already knew almost everything that I was being taught about nutrition, and most of what they were teaching me about wellness. I knew it all, but hadn't been practicing it. I had been doing things my way instead of following God's will for my well-being. It occurred to me that this might be the reason I was now in the position I was in.

At Hartland, when I examined the NEW START acronym, God showed me my downfall:

Nutrition. The extent of my fruit consumption (per day) had generally been ONE apple or ONE orange. For vegetables, I'd been consuming one small salad a day and/or maybe a couple servings of vegetables. I loved fried foods, even though every nutritional book points out that they're the most difficult foods to digest — very hard on the system.

Exercise. When I'd moved to Maryland, I simply stopped getting my routine forty-five-minute exercise sessions.

Water! Plain, fresh, water: When and why had I stopped drinking my two-liter bottle of water? Let's see...When we'd moved to Maryland, I had allowed the "strange" taste and smell of even filtered Maryland water to discourage me from keeping my body well flushed and hydrated. Thank you, Lord, for the change that has now come over me! Every day, I'm drinking at least eight ounces of water per every twenty pounds of body weight.

Sunshine, temperance, and fresh air. Ha! For years I'd been burning the candle at both ends and in the middle! So my paradigm went something like this: "What choice do I have? As mother, pastor's wife, and Pathfinder Leader, it's amazing I find time for a full-time job!" In the winter, it's hard to get outside, and I certainly didn't intend to make an extra effort to get my fifteen minutes of quality sunlight and Vitamin D3.

Rest. This has always been — and still is — a challenge for me.

Trust in God was — and is — a steady journey and a joy!

The Hartland experience clearly showed me that I did (and do) have choices, and that many of my choices had been self-destructive. Society has a way of turning our attention toward things that do not endorse NEW START. Unless God's people are intentional in rejecting unhealthy foods and habits, we'll be doing the same thing everybody else is doing (even though everybody else is going down the wrong road)! Besides providing us with the Way to salvation, I believe that God created this earth with everything we need for maintaining good health.

After learning from the Hartland staff that my post-treatment blood work showed tremendous improvement, I returned home with a renewed lease on life and a new attitude. By God's power, I maintained what I had practiced at Hartland. Knowing how critical it is to ask God daily for the baptism of His Holy Spirit, I prayed without ceasing — talking with God during daylight hours more than I ever had before. And the family was diligent in not allowing time to get away from us; we made a concerted effort to maintain the family worship routine.

November rolled around, and my oncologist's office wrote prescriptions for me to have a slew of tests done before my follow-up appointment. I finished my scans and lab tests, and went to see him.

After he physically examined me, he said, "You look very good. You look very healthy! And that's not all, Brenda. All of your lab reports and all of your scans have come back clean as a whistle." (HALLELUJAH!) "Whatever you're doing, keep it up! But I want to see you again in six months."

For three years, I continued to drink my healing herbal teas. And for three years, I went through a battery of tests — every six months — followed by a visit to my oncologist. His report was always the same:

"Clean as a whistle!" At the end of the fourth and fifth years, I faithfully returned for checkups. The cancer never returned!

I just give God all the honor and all the glory! This experience made me realize that God had supplied — from the very beginning — the things He knew we needed to stay healthy. It wasn't until I went to Hartland that I really paid attention to the creation story. There was an order to the sequence of creating the world and its inhabitants. Everything that God created was designed perfectly to accommodate the full benefit of what was coming next. From the very beginning, God had provided fruits, nuts, and grains for "meat" (food). Who am I to change this? I believe — without question — that God used the original human diet (a plant-based diet) and the abundance of live (raw) foods and healing herbs to cure my illness.

Having received my miracle, I decided that I needed to take the advice of the Master. Jesus once told a tender, beloved soul to "go, and sin no more." I took this message to heart. I realized that I could not return to the lifestyle I'd had prior to my healing. There could be no more dairy, eggs, potato chips and French fries, etc.

By God's grace, I have maintained a wellness lifestyle, including a substantial, well-balanced plant-based meal to start each day — breakfast! And by God's grace, I have remained cancer free!

The Story of
Lee Forbes

As told by Lee

I was born in the mid-1950s in the city of Raleigh, North Carolina. My mother had given birth to one child previously, a stillborn. My father was a bus driver. We worshiped with the Southern Baptists until I was eleven years old. Baptized at the age of eight, I believed in God, and I felt like I had a personal relationship with Him. Generally speaking, I was a very good boy, as long as I was spanked on regular occasions. I had wonderful parents and grew up in a very loving home. I was a very strong-willed child but typically, my desire was to please my parents and other people. In the old South, when you were told what to do, you did it. If you were told what not to do, and you did it anyway, you were treated to the paddle or the belt, which helped to remind you what you wanted to do the next time.

I remember very clearly — one of the things that was so difficult for me, even though I was in Sunday School and church and hearing regularly about the love of God, was kneeling down by my bed and praying every night. Typically, it was, "Now I lay me down to sleep. I pray thee, Lord, my soul to keep. If I should die before I wake, I pray thee, Lord, my soul to take." Every time I got to the last part, I remember thinking, "Death means there will be a race between God and Satan." And if I had been good enough that day, God was going to be a little bit faster. If I hadn't been, the devil would have the upper hand. Every night, because of my strong-willed nature, I realized it may have been a close race. This meant that if the devil got to me first, I was going to be writhing in eternal torment for the rest of my life.

That battle went on in my child's heart for many years until, at age twelve, we moved to Salisbury, Maryland, and we joined the Seventh-day Adventist Church. I was re-baptized at the age of thirteen. It was shown to us in the scriptures that when we die, we just rest in the grave until Jesus comes back. That was probably one of the biggest turning points in my born-again experience (or I should say, "boosting points") because then I knew for sure that God really loved me, and that only the righteous will live eternally! The unrighteous do not live eternally. Nevertheless, unfortunately, I cannot say that I was a great person from that day onward.

I went to Highland View Academy in Hagerstown, Maryland. During my senior year, I became certified as a SCUBA diver. After graduation, I spent two years as a commercial diver in Ocean City, Maryland. As spring became summer, I found myself at a camp meeting in Hagerstown. On the way home, Saturday night, I had a severe earache, so I stopped at the Adventist Hospital in Takoma Park. The physician said I had a perforated eardrum, and referred me to a specialist. The next week, I went to see an ear, nose, and throat specialist in Salisbury. Upon examination of my ear, he used some superlatives about a cholesteatoma in my middle ear. He said, "There's a tumor attached to the mastoid process in your skull, and it looks like it is about five years advanced. If you don't have major surgery soon, it will continue to eat through the bone into your brain until you become deaf, blind, and you eventually die." He scheduled an audiogram for me. They found that I had lost 60% of my hearing in my left ear.

The surgery for cholesteatoma in those days was highly invasive and could potentially handicap me in many ways. I would not be able to handle pressure changes, not even driving up in the mountains. I would not be able to go swimming, take showers, or be able to bear loud noises. Here I was, an 18-year-old young man, basically just beginning my life. So the following week, I went through consultation concerning my future. What kind of work might I get involved in? What would my limitations be? It was quite a shock. But that following weekend, I shared my problem with my friends at camp.

The next weekend when I went to church, my mother asked me, "Have you considered being anointed and having people pray for you?"

I said I hadn't really thought about it, but I was reminded of the book of James, chapter five, where it says, "Is any among you afflicted? Is any sick among you? Let him call for the elders of the church, and let them pray over him, anointing him with oil in the name of the Lord: and the prayer of faith shall save the sick, and the Lord shall raise him up." So I decided, "Yes. I would like to be anointed."

An elder from another church was visiting us, so we asked him, Pastor Murphy, and another elder to join us. The three of them, along with my mother and me, went to a back room (after the service) for the anointing. We all knelt together. Pastor Murphy had a small bottle of olive oil, and he put a drop of it on my ear and a drop on my forehead. Then they all laid hands on me and simply asked God to heal me.

I didn't feel anything immediately. No bright lights; no overwhelming surge of energy through my body. But I had the confidence that whatever God wanted, that would be the case.

We went home and had lunch. I just lay down on the couch and went to sleep. My mother said I slept deeper than she had ever seen me sleep. I never moved; I was perfectly still for three hours. During that time they were singing and playing the piano, having music in the living room. After three hours, she woke me up. I woke up with a loud ringing inside my head and my left ear. It would not go away!

I had to go to work on Sunday morning. Ordinarily, I worked as a diver, but because of my ear problem, I went to work in the welding shop. It was particularly loud...surface grinders and mallets hitting metal. Yet, above all that noise, I could still hear this ringing in my ear. So that evening, I called the physician at his home and told him about the ringing. He said, "I have no idea what it could be. However," he told me, "I'll be going out of town for a few days' vacation, so I can examine you before I go, if you can come to my office first thing tomorrow morning."

I got there 9:00 a.m., Monday morning. First he looked in my good ear. "Everything looks fine here," he said. Then he examined my left ear. Looking somewhat puzzled, he picked up a small probe and another instrument. Next, I heard something that sounded like a small vacuum cleaner. After a couple minutes, he turned it off, looked very strangely at me, and blurted, "You have healed yourself!"

"Praise God!" I exclaimed.

"You can praise whoever you want to. I have never seen anything like this in my life!" He continued, "The sound you heard when I vacuumed your ear canal was the sound of the tumor fragments being removed. The mass had shriveled up, and it was just sitting there deep inside your ear. The scar looks like it's about two months old. I have never ever seen anything like this in my life." Then he took me to the sound booth and tested the hearing in my left ear. It was better than in my right ear! Since that time, I've had numerous examinations. There is no scar tissue at all. The healing was perfect! Thank You, Lord Jesus!

I have been involved in many anointings over the years. In some, I have seen people miraculously healed. Others were not healed. But in every situation, the people were at peace with whatever God chose. That, I think, was the most important part because their hearts and their souls were healed, and they realized that God had for them what was best—salvation! After my healing at age eighteen, I was very thankful to God. Yet, I still fell back into some of the old ways following some examples that were not so good.

I thought I might find a job I was better suited for, so I moved to North Carolina, where I started working as a carpenter's helper. The foreman was also a Seventh-day Adventist, so we had a great relationship. One day we were working outside on a condominium project. A four-story scaffolding had to be taken down. There was a 4 x 4 plywood platform at the top. He told me to climb one side of the scaffolding, and he would go up on the other side. We were five or six bucks in the air. We were just going to push this platform off, and then start taking the bucks apart. The back legs of the scaffolding were standing on three cinderblocks, and the front legs were standing on the steps to the building entrance.

When we threw the platform off, the back legs buckled under! The only direction in which the scaffolding could fall was away from the building. We were thirty feet in the air when it started to fall. Then suddenly, for no discernible reason, the scaffolding changed direction and began to fall towards the building — falling down the face of the building. As it was falling, I caught hold of a railing on the second floor balcony. I just hung there watching it fall towards the foreman. There was no conceivable way he could escape. He managed to drop down one block. (It looked like the fall was going to crush him!) Miraculously, he landed in a garbage pile of broken boards, plywood and cardboard. The top section of the scaffolding separated and shot out over his head. The man actually walked out of that pile of trash without a scratch! I was able to drop down to a lower balcony, and I, too, walked away. It was only the hand of God that caused that scaffolding to fall back the other way, injuring neither one of us.

Soon after that experience, I again decided there must be a better way to make a living, so I got involved in emergency medical training. I became one of the first paramedics in North Carolina. Living in Tyron (in the Columbus area of western North Carolina) I worked for St. Luke's Hospital. As a hospital-based paramedic, I had many opportunities to get involved in the diverse medical care of many people. Although I enjoyed the work, I took some jobs on the side for a roofing company to make extra money. Later I moved to Asheville, North Carolina, and began my own business as a roofing contractor.

I was working on a project and standing on a ladder in a warehouse, fourteen feet up in the air. I was a young man in my thirties. One of the non-skid pads on the bottom of the ladder had come off. I was not aware of it, or I just didn't pay any attention to it. Suddenly, the ladder just slipped out from under me and dropped me those fourteen feet. Halfway down, I hit a steel bar — centered it with my left knee. That broke the kneecap in half. Then my leg recoiled before I hit the concrete, so I took the fall on that lower half of the patella, crushing the bone at its lower edge. As I was lying there in intense agony, I placed my hand on my knee, and with my middle finger I could feel the two halves of my patella. I was in severe pain and thinking about the time it would take before I could get any pain killers. I prayed, "Lord, please either take the pain away, or give me the strength to bear it." Within two minutes, the pain was gone! I had no pain! When the paramedics got there, my knee was so badly swollen, they couldn't tell for sure if it was broken (aside from the fact that the leg was slightly twisted). On the way to the hospital, I was joking and carrying on with everyone so much that no one believed my kneecap was broken. When we got to the hospital, the x-ray technician remarked, "It's not broken. It's just dislocated."

I said, "Oh no. It is broken!"

The technician argued with me, so I said, "I will bet you on it."

She said. "It couldn't be 'cause you wouldn't be carrying on like that if it was really broken."

I answered, "I prayed, and God took the pain away."

When she looked at the x-ray, she came back with a blank expression on her face and said, "It's really broken!"

Well, praise the Lord! I didn't have any pain from that moment until I came out of surgery at 10 o'clock that night. That was September, 1985, in Memorial Mission Hospital in Asheville, North Carolina. The physician, Dr. Larry Kroll, removed part of the patella and put two screws in the remainder of that bone. I've never had any trouble with that knee. The only time it gets the least bit sore is when I've been climbing ladders all day long. Weather has never been a problem. I climb; I repel; I hike. God has just been so good to me healing my broken body. Along with my healings has come spiritual growth.

Station WPEK, in Asheville, was one of those news/talk stations I enjoyed listening to. One day, I asked them to have someone come out and talk to me about advertising my business on the radio. At that point, my business was very well established, but I really wanted to support the station and the work they were doing. During a conversation with the sales rep, I asked him, just out of curiosity, "What does it cost to host a program on the radio?" I was thinking about a program where people could call in and ask questions, and I could give them answers with Bible references.

He said, "I don't know, but I'll talk to the station manager and I'll get back to you."

I was looking forward to his call because I had been traveling with a self-supporting ministry nationally and internationally, holding conferences on how to study the Bible, memorization techniques, etc.

Later that week, the sales rep called me and said, "Lee, I have an advertising package for you. We would like you to consider doing a Sunday morning program, like we discussed, from 8 to 9 o'clock."

Wow! That's the golden hour, prime time, when people are getting ready for Sunday School. So I called my friend, Clark Floyd, and said, "Clark, we're going to be on the radio!"

He said, "You're kidding."

"No. I'm serious. We start next week." God had opened that door wide!

So we started the program on station WPEK, 880 AM, and it was a success! People called us during the program with all kinds of questions, and people even called after the program was over. They'd say, "We were enjoying your program, and we didn't want to interrupt."

One gentleman called and said, "My wife, my children, and I sit around the breakfast table every Sunday morning, listening to your program. We love hearing what you're sharing from the Bible."

I advertised my business a little during the program, but after three months, I hadn't received an invoice. I asked the sales manager, "Where is the invoice for my advertising?"

He said, "The manager likes your program so much, we're not charging you anything for it. We are just making Bible Answers a part of our programming." So we had this free program during the golden hour on Sunday morning. We had a wonderful time, and developed a tremendous rapport with the community.

One day, when I happened to be at the station, the manager stopped me. He said, "Lee, the accounts department hasn't been charging you for the program, have they?"

I said, "No. I understand you just wanted us to be part of your programming, and you were not going to charge us anything."

He said, "That's right. I was just double-checking. We really like the program. We get good feedback. Although," he hesitated. "I am a reformed Presbyterian. Last Sunday, when I got to church, the deacons were waiting for me on the front steps. They asked me, very seriously, 'Did you hear what they were teaching on your station a couple weeks ago?'"

"I said, 'No, I didn't.' So they proceeded to tell me what you had been saying."

"I asked them, 'Did you call the program to challenge them?'"

"They said, 'No.'"

"Why not?"

"Because they were using the Bible!"

We both laughed, and then he told me, "Whatever you are doing, Lee, just keep on doing it because I really like it!"

It was truly a miracle that God set that up for us because it was nothing we had ever planned on doing, or even talked about. It was tremendous fun while it lasted from March, 1999 until March, 2001. The only reason we stopped was because Clear Channel bought the station and didn't want any noncommercial programming on the station.

Growing in grace and the knowledge of Jesus Christ over the decades, I have been blessed with continued success in my business. On April 24, 2011, I was looking at a slate roof that needed some repairs in White Sulfur Springs, West Virginia. Joshua, one of my employees, was with me. We were walking around on the roof, looking at the damage, and estimating the needed repairs. I examined a bracket where we would have to tie in the safety rope. Bending forward to go down on my knees, my feet slid out from under me! There was nothing I could do. All the tread had worn off my shoes. I slid on my stomach (about six feet) while trying to catch myself on the snow stops. I missed all except one, which caught my breastbone and broke five of my ribs and my sternum! Then my left foot hit the edge of the gutter. It spun me around in mid-air. I slammed into a rock wall, fell about twelve feet, and landed on my head in the dirt. Joshua, on the other side of the roof, hadn't seen me fall. But when he came down the ladder, he saw me headfirst in the dirt with my body crumpled over me. He ran over to me and said, "Lee, can you move your arms and legs?" I was paralyzed. I couldn't move anything!

Joshua immediately called 911, and when they heard that it was a neck injury, they called Beckley to have the MedEvac helicopter meet me at White Sulfur Springs. When the paramedics arrived, they had to clear out some bushes so they could get me onto a hardboard stretcher and carry me to the ambulance. The ambulance drove me down to a landing place for the helicopter. By then, the helicopter was just coming in for a landing. (A pilot myself, I'd always wanted to fly in a helicopter.) As we were lifting off, the pilot asked me, "Do you want to go to Charleston or Roanoke?"

I said, " Roanoke." By 6 o'clock, they were delivering me to the emergency room at the Carilion Roanoke Memorial Hospital in Virginia.

At the hospital, they immediately took x-rays, CAT scans, and an MRI. I had four broken vertebrae in my neck. One of the discs was pushed out in such an extreme way that the spinal cord was being compressed. By that time, I was getting feeling back in my arms and legs. I was able to move my legs a fair amount, but my arms — only a very little. The pain was really minimal — not as excruciating as I had anticipated. Breathing did not hurt. Anyone who has ever had broken ribs knows how excruciatingly painful it can be when you're breathing, especially when you're breathing deep. My shoulder (that had landed against the rock wall) probably ached the most, although there was nothing broken. I did have extensive bruising on my back and my right side (where I'd hit the wall on the way down). The next day, I had surgery. They had to fuse four vertebrae in my neck. Initially, the doctor told me that with the type of injury I had sustained, I would be in the hospital for two or three weeks. Then I would be in rehab from four to six weeks before starting rehab at home.

You know, the amazing thing about being involved in ministry and having wonderful Christian friends is that they know the Source of healing. I had people praying for me all over the world. I received letters and phone calls. I was so touched. I shed a lot of tears because so many people cared enough to be praying for me, constantly.

My wife is the bookkeeper for a ministerial association in Alderson. She was in a meeting with her phone turned off, and didn't hear about my accident until an hour afterwards. The meeting was in a church, and by the time she found out, everybody was heading out. She immediately called all the ministers to let them know what had happened. There just happened to be (right then in the sanctuary) a little prayer group. Immediately, they started praying for my healing and my survival. She didn't even know if I would still be alive when she got to me! Because it was a three-hour drive to Roanoke from our home, she had to find someone to watch our three girls. She finally got in touch with her mother, but her mom got lost on the way to our house, so by the time she got to the hospital, it was midnight. On the way there, she wondered if I'd live, and if I'd be paralyzed from the neck down. She just told the Lord, "Whatever You choose, God, I know You will prepare me for it." He prepared her for my huge black eye. I was not a pretty sight. But I was far prettier then all she had imagined.

Those "three weeks" and "six weeks" turned out to be only seventeen days total. Eight days after I was admitted to the hospital, I was moved to rehab, and nine days later, I was sent home. Because I was progressing so well, I attributed it to the prayers of all the precious people out there. God, again, had healed me quickly in His supernatural time. Each step I take, I believe, is a miracle.

Recently, my supplier told me about another roofing contractor who'd just fallen off a roof — nine feet, headfirst! After four days, they took him off life support. So it's a miracle that I'm alive, and it's a miracle I'm not paralyzed. Falling nine to twelve feet headfirst is typically not recommended. I still plan to get back on a roof as soon as I'm able. I'm getting more stable all the time, and I'm regaining my strength. Yes, I know I'm hardheaded. (When I was growing up, my dad always called me "knothead" or "bonehead.") But I trust God, and I trust His perfect love, which casts out all fear. I've seen so many miraculous ways that God has delivered me.

Now I'm just asking the Lord what He wants me to do with the rest of my life. I am open. I've been a lay minister for years. I've become involved with a local Baptist Church. I began teaching Sunday school there. They then assigned me as an interim minister. Although I am a Seventh-day Adventist, I guess I'm a Southern Baptist Seventh-day Adventist. Primarily, I'm just a Christian who is very focused on scriptural truths, sharing that with people, and teaching them about scriptural prophecy. I pray that God has something even more planned for me in ministry.

About the Author

G. Warren Sears was the right person to compile this book. For the past sixty years, Warren's life has prepared him in several ways for the job at hand.

A WWII veteran, Warren gave his heart to God in 1953. Ever since, he has sought to convince people that Jesus Christ is truly Who the Bible says He is. Jesus said, "I am the resurrection, and the life: he that believeth in Me, though he were dead, yet shall he live: and whosoever liveth and believeth in Me shall never die." (John 11:25 KJV) In his first book, "Adventures of a Witness for Jesus," Warren offers creative ideas on sharing with others the love, joy, and power of knowing the God of the universe.

About thirteen years ago, Warren was hit with a type of cancer that was so rare that his doctors were not sure how to treat it. One evening, Warren was invited to a dinner meeting where the speaker told several stories about God using him to pray for people. Warren asked for prayer. Three days later all his symptoms were gone! So he knows firsthand the power of praying to Doctor Jesus.

When George Cupp first told Warren about George, Jr.'s accident and miraculous healing, God placed on Warren's heart the urge to write this book. At first, he felt incapable of doing the job. One day, Wendy Agard visited his church. The moment Warren met her, he heard God say, "She will help you write the book." Wendy is not only an excellent proofreader, she is also a registered nurse. She was a tremendous help to Warren, throughout.

Warren's prayer is that God will touch the heart of every one who reads this book. They will be convinced that Jesus is truly the Son of God and they will open their heart to receive Him and make Him the Lord of their life. Confess your sins to God. He forgave you when Jesus paid for your sins on Calvary's cross. That is the key to being born again by the Holy Spirit—and getting onto the path of eternal life. Then, attend a church that teaches the Bible is the Word of Life, and get ready for the Lord's soon return. Amen.

A personal note from Warren

Dear Reader:

If you enjoyed reading this book, then please tell your pastor, youth leader, teachers, and activity directors.

I welcome all opportunities to speak to any gathering where the marvelous work of Doctor Jesus is the prime focus. For example: church banquets, luncheons, dinner meetings, evangelism seminars, and any events where the saints gather. I teach, motivate, and encourage Christians to be fearless, effective, and joyful witnesses for the Lord.

The joy of the Lord is my strength.

Warren

✎

ENDORSEMENTS WANTED

If you enjoyed this book, write a few lines for my new website to tell others. Email your endorsement to: Gwarrensears@gmail.com

TO ORDER BOOKS

Order from the publisher: BOOKS@yav.com

Order signed copies direct from the author: 888-729-4280

BOOK STORES: Please order from Ingram

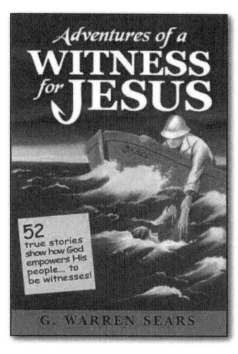

GOOD NEWS

Warren's most popular book is now available as an

E-BOOK

ONLY **$2.99**
at Amazon

52 true stories show how God empowers His people…to be witnesses!

These stories, selected from Warren's journals, show how God works today in a wide variety of situations. Although prayer and dependence upon the Holy Spirit is still the master plan for leading lost souls to a wonderful Savior, this book will give you fresh ideas and new concepts that make witnessing a win-win ministry. You will learn, by example, how to:

- ♦ overcome the fear of witnessing to strangers
- ♦ avoid arguing about doctrinal stuff
- ♦ speak the truth in love
- ♦ effectively share your testimony
- ♦ present God's plan of salvation
- ♦ use the Romans Road gospel verses
- ♦ lead the sinner in a salvation prayer

The original paperback edition is available at bookstores, now specially priced at US$10.95.

Book stores: Please order from Ingram or contact the publisher: Books@yav.com